SUCCESSFUL WARMUPS, BOOK 1

By Nancy Telfer

ISBN O - 8497 - 4174 - 2

CONTENTS

	Page
First Year Warmups	3
First Year Progress Chart	47
Second Year Warmups	49
Second Year Progress Chart	93
Index	95

Making the Most of Your Warmups:

1) Always warm up your voice before or at the beginning of a rehearsal.
2) Start with the first five warmups in this book (1a to 1e). Use these five for one week. Then omit Warmup 1a and add Warmup 2. Each week continue to omit the oldest warmup and add the next new one so that you always have five warmups to practice.
3) Use the tips to make the most of each warmup.
4) At the end of each week, check off the warmups you have been using:

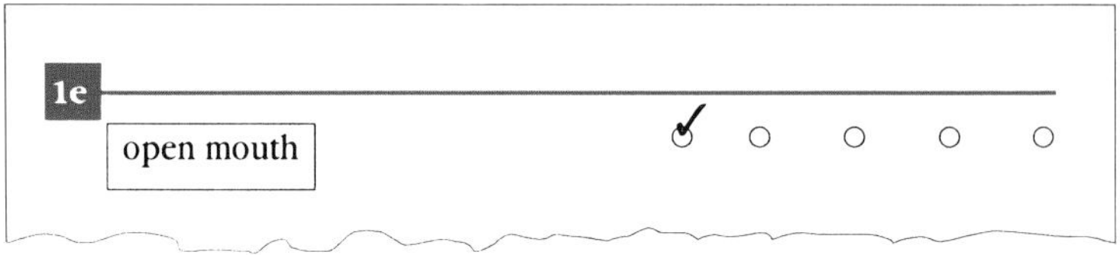

Then circle the appropriate numbers on the progress chart.

5) If you are eager to improve in some specific area, check the index for appropriate warmups.

Soloists: In warmups with more than one vocal part, you may choose the part with the best range for your voice or change the key.

Men's, Women's and Children's Choirs: See the Conductor's Edition for special instructions.

First Year

Each voice is unique: a gift to explore and develop.

SINGERS IN POSITION

Stand in a balanced position prepared for good singing.

Correct:

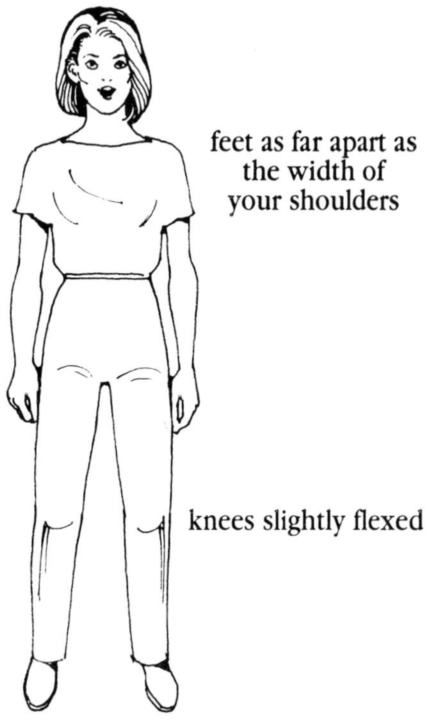

Incorrect:

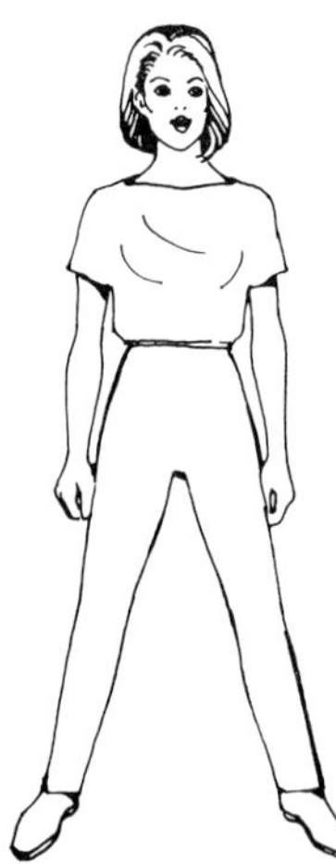

legs too far apart
(not flexible)

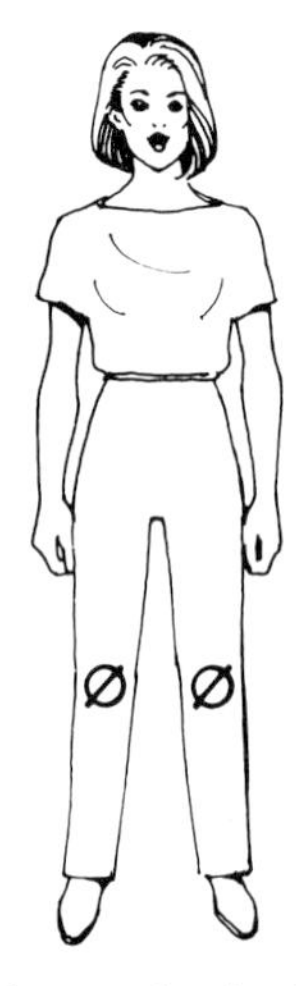

knees locked
(not flexible)

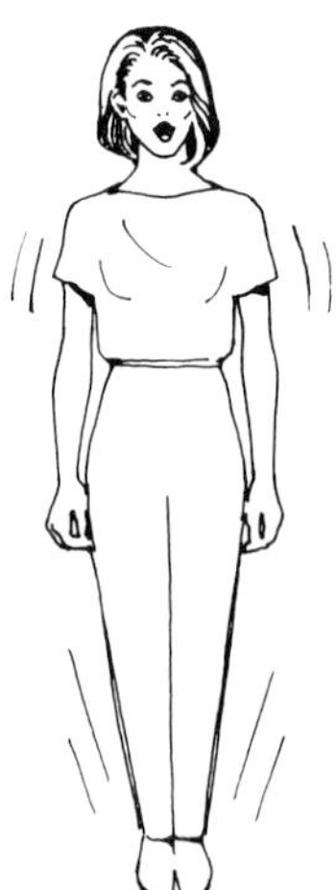

feet touching
(tippy)

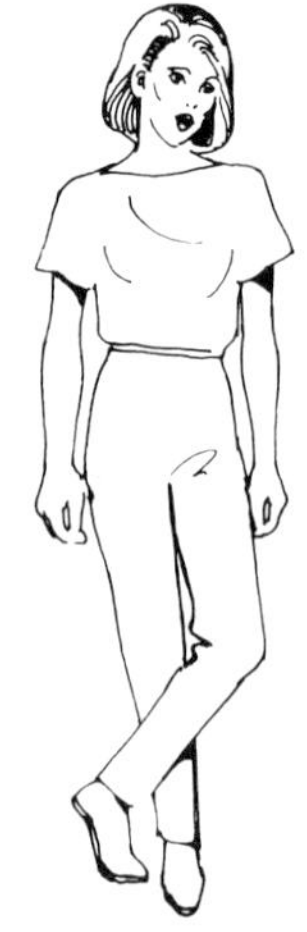

weight on one leg
(off-balance)

1a

building muscles for breath support

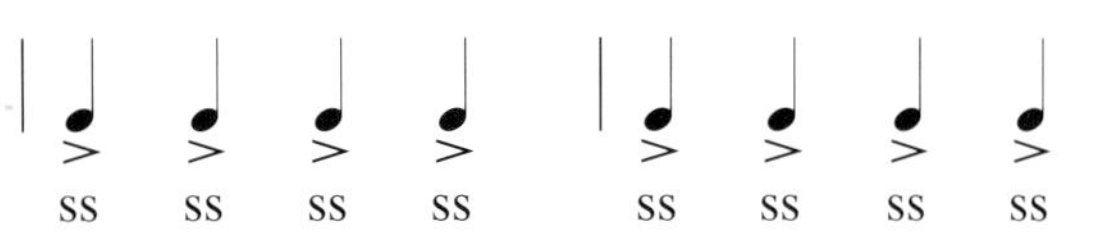

Breathe 2 3 4

ss ss ss ss ss ss ss ss

TIPS

A. Breathe quietly through your mouth. A deep breath will relax your body.

B. Make one small, quick bounce out with your tummy for each accent.

C. Try omitting the accents. Make all the hisses even:

1b

b p ; working the lips

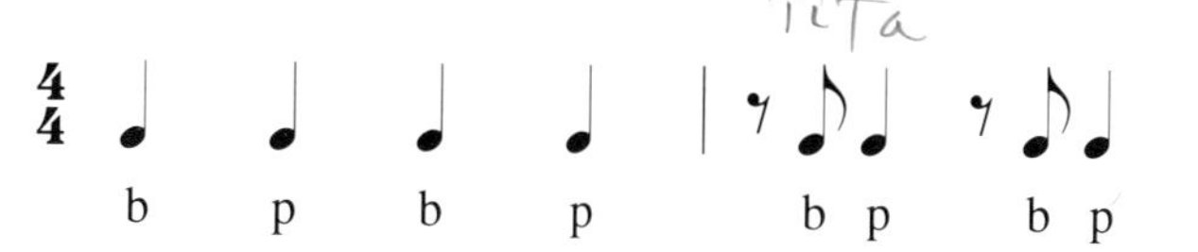

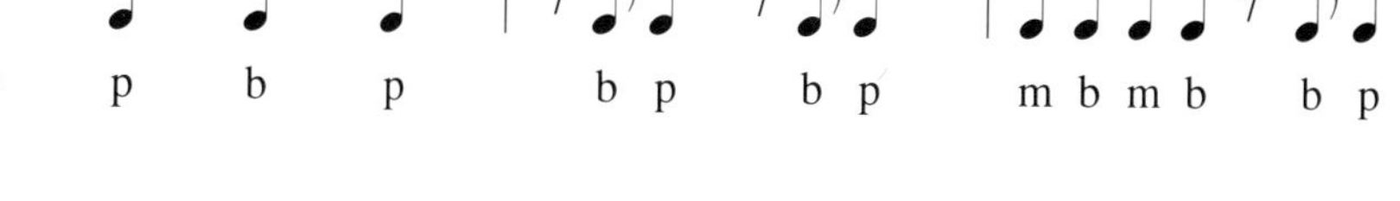

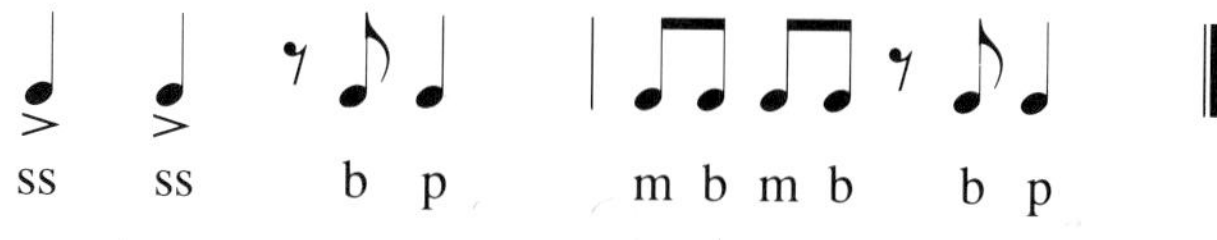

TIPS

A. Your lips should be in almost the same position for “b” and “p.”

B. Keep an even beat.

C. Do the accent from your tummy.

short consonants; long vowels

○ ○ ○

Legato (♩ = 72)

Breathe 2

Bah bah bah bah bah bah bah;

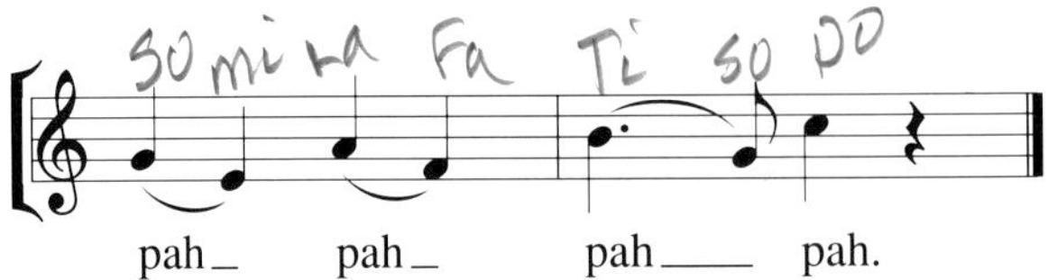

pah_ pah_ pah___ pah.

TIPS

A. Think: short consonants, long vowels.

B. Place the vowel right on the beat:

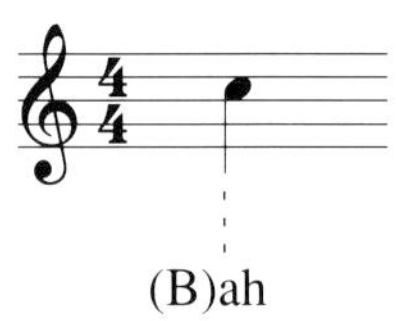

(B)ah

C. Sing each phrase with a continuous sound (no space between notes):

1d

ah: tone quality

○ ○ ○

Very slowly (♩ = 56 - 69)

Breathe 2

Ah ___

TIPS

A. Open your mouth north/south, not east/west.

correct:

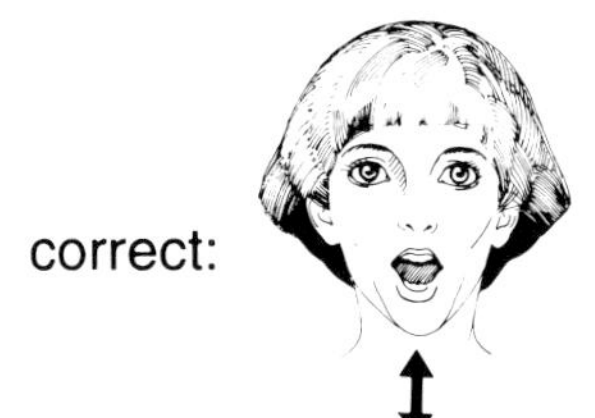

incorrect:

B. Think of the vowel as a circle of sound.

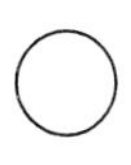

piano

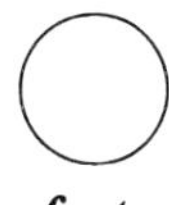

forte

1e

open mouth

Andante (♩ = 84)

Part 1
Part 2

Yum yum yum yum yah, yum yum yum yum yah,

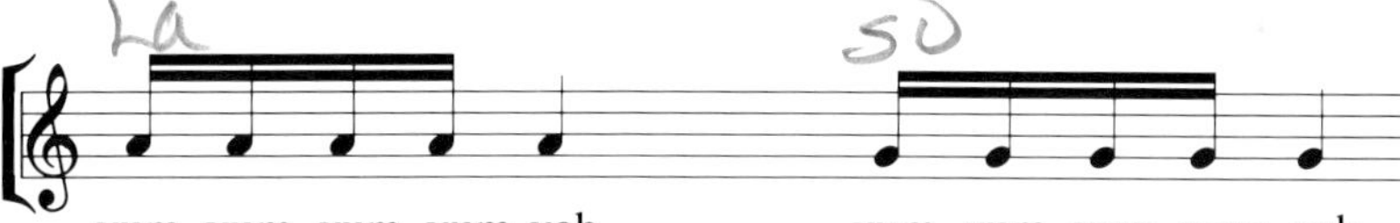

yum yum yum yum yah, yum yum yum yum yah,

yum yum yum yum yah, yum yum yum yum yah,

yum yum yum yum yah, yum yum yum yum yah.

TIPS

A. Exaggerate the "m."

B. Drop your jaw down suddenly for "yah."

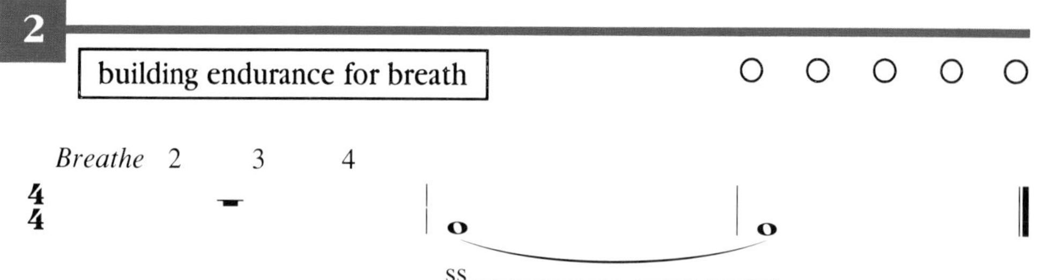

TIPS

A. Feel your tummy expand as you breathe in.
B. Shoulders should stay relaxed and down.
C. Listen for a steady hiss.

SINGERS IN POSITION

Hold your book so that you can see the conductor and the music without moving your head up and down.

Correct:

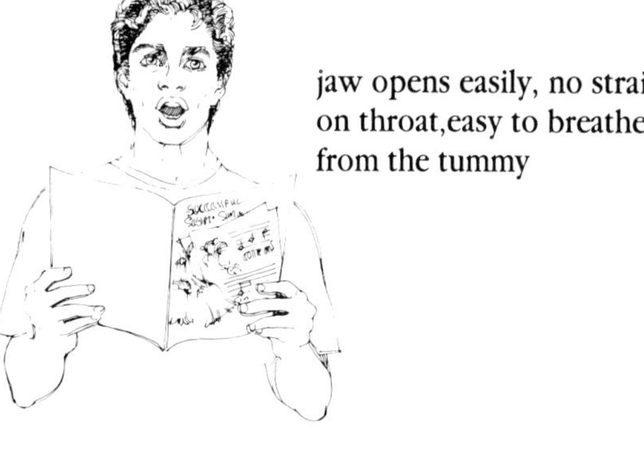

jaw opens easily, no strain on throat,easy to breathe from the tummy

Incorrect:

constricted throat, ribs pushing on tummy

throat tightly stretched

When you are not singing, you may hold the music at a lower level.

3

d t j ; working the tongue

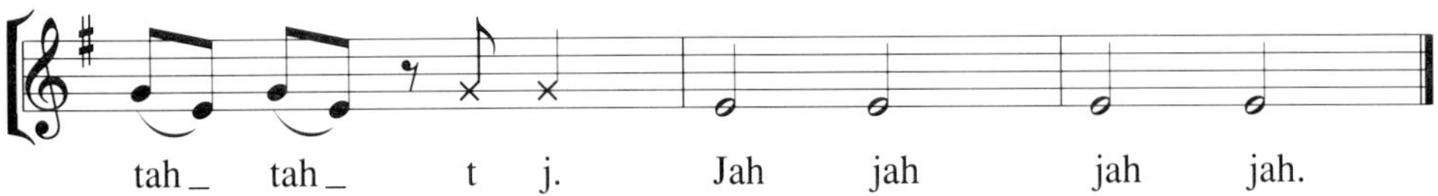

TIPS

A. Move the tip of your tongue quickly and lightly for "t" and "j."

B. For a healthy voice, drink plenty of water each day.

4

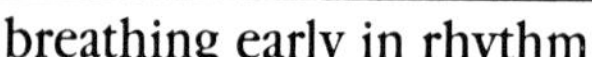
breathing early in rhythm

(= 76 - 96)
Sop. Breathe 2 3 4; prepare 2 3 4
Dah_ dah dah_ dah
Alto
Dah dah
Tenor
Dah_ dah dah_ dah
Bass
Dah dah

Breathe 2 3 4
dah_ dah dah dah dah dah dah.
dah dah dah dah.
dah_ dah dah dah dah dah dah.
dah dah_ dah_ dah.

Dah_ dah dah_ dah dah_ dah dah dah dah dah
Dah dah dah dah dah
Dah_ dah dah_ dah dah_ dah dah dah dah dah
Dah dah dah dah_ dah_

Breathe 2
dah_ dah. Dah dah dah dah_ dah
dah dah dah. Dah dah_ dah
dah dah dah. Dah dah
dah. Dah dah

Breathe
dah dah dah dah.
Dah dah dah dah
dah dah.
Dah dah
dah dah.
Dah dah dah dah
dah dah.
Dah dah

dah dah dah dah dah dah dah.
dah dah dah dah dah.
dah dah dah dah dah dah dah dah.
dah dah dah dah.

TIPS

A. **Feel the beats as you breathe in.**

B. **During the "prepare," feel the air pressure in your tummy. Then sing out with a steady stream of air.**

C. **There should be no sudden burst of air as you begin to sing.**

D. **Take just the amount of air you need. Release all the air by the end of each phrase.**

Breathe
Prepare
Sing
(Air all gone)
PRESSURE

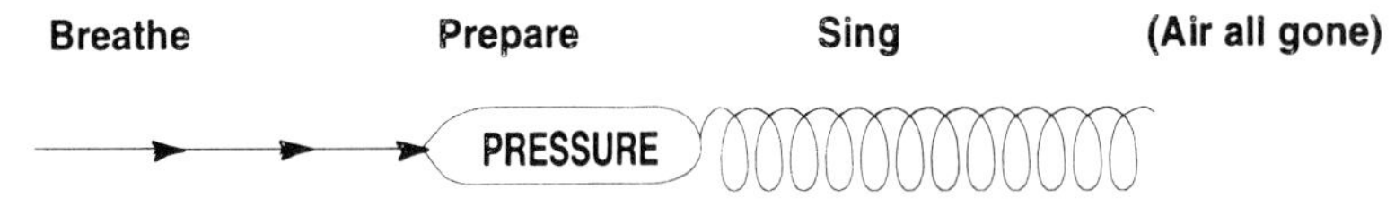

SINGERS IN POSITION

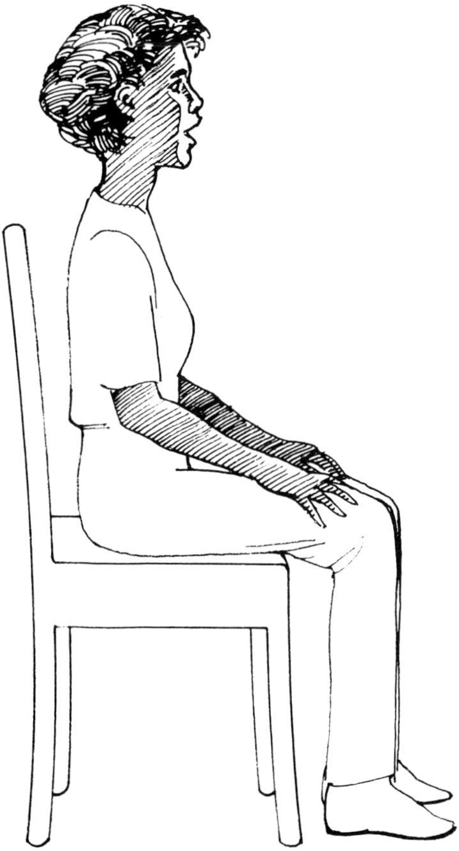

back straight,
not touching
the chair
sit "hard on the bones"
feet flat on floor,
ready to stand
no crossed legs or ankles

steady beat

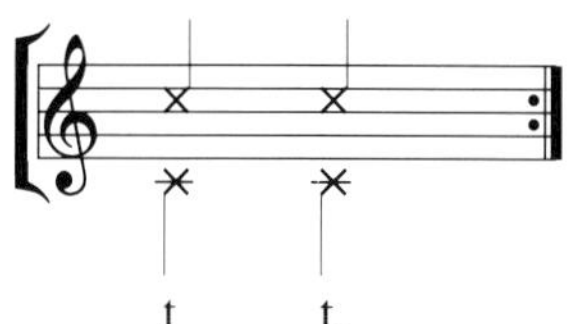

TIPS

A. Keep your posture balanced.

B. Place the “t” of “plate” on the first beat of the next bar.

C. Feel the beat from within. Do not tap your toe or hand.

BREATHING

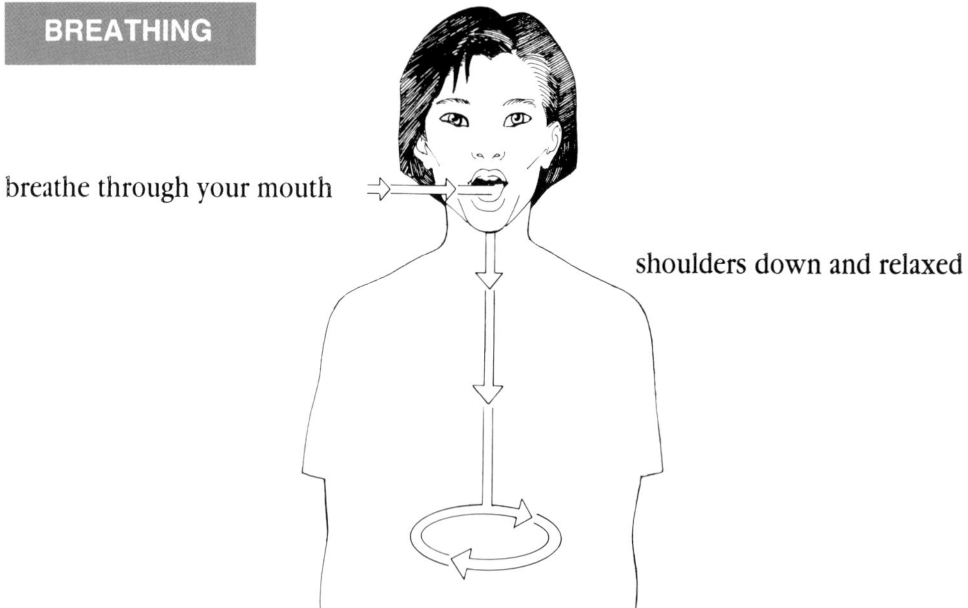

breathe in until the air fills up the front and then the back of the abdomen

6

tuning repeated pitches

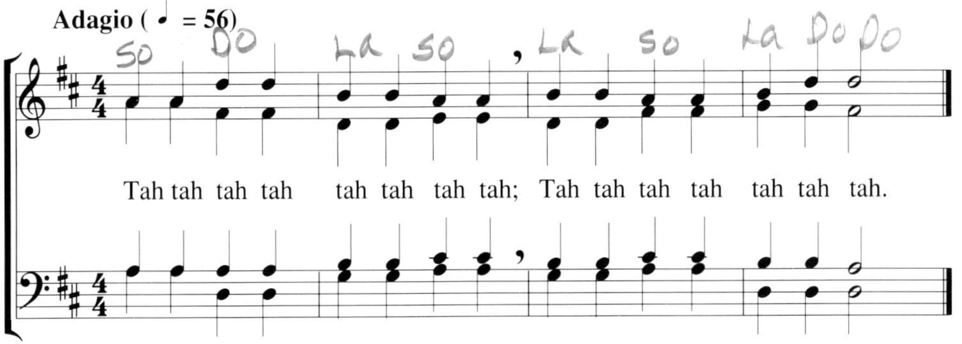

TIPS

A. Keep the sound flowing forward.

B. Listen carefully to the tuning of each repeated pitch.

7

ee

TIPS

A. For "ee," keep your mouth open north/south.

B. Keep the jaw relaxed. When you change from "tah" to "ee," the tongue will move slightly but the jaw should remain in the same position.

REMINDER **Balance your body; keep your shoulders down.**

8

m ; forward placement of the voice

○ ○ ○ ○ ○

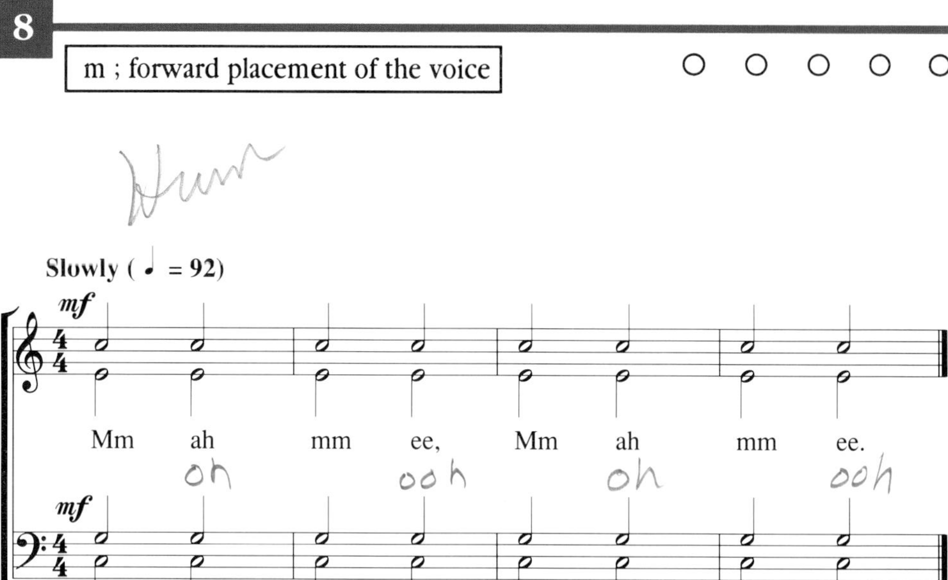

TIPS

A. For "m," keep your lips relaxed and teeth slightly apart.

B. Let the buzz (resonance) of the "m" go forward into the vowel.

C. Humming is one of the fastest ways to warm up your voice.

9

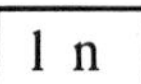

TIPS

A. Flip the "l" quickly with the tongue.
B. Let the "n" buzz. Your tongue should tickle.
C. To keep from going flat, think "up" as the pitch descends.

REMINDER Open your mouth north/south.

10

open throat

○ ○ ○ ○ ○

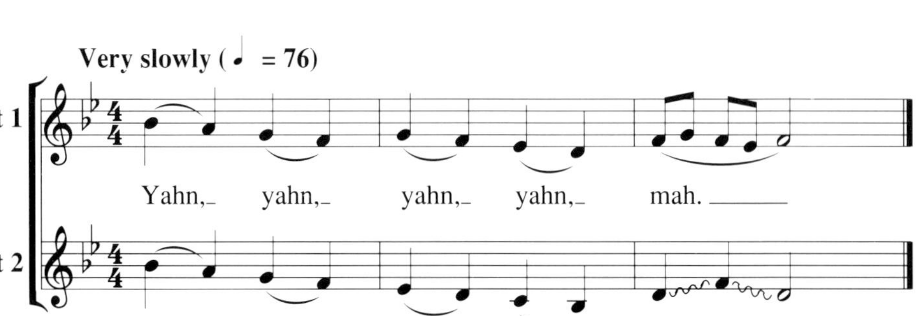

TIPS

A. Feel your throat relax lazily on each "yahn."
B. Stretch out the "m" on "mah."
C. Imagine an orange, then a grapefruit, then a watermelon in your throat. Feel the huge opening.

11

emphasizing the main beat

○ ○ ○ ○ ○

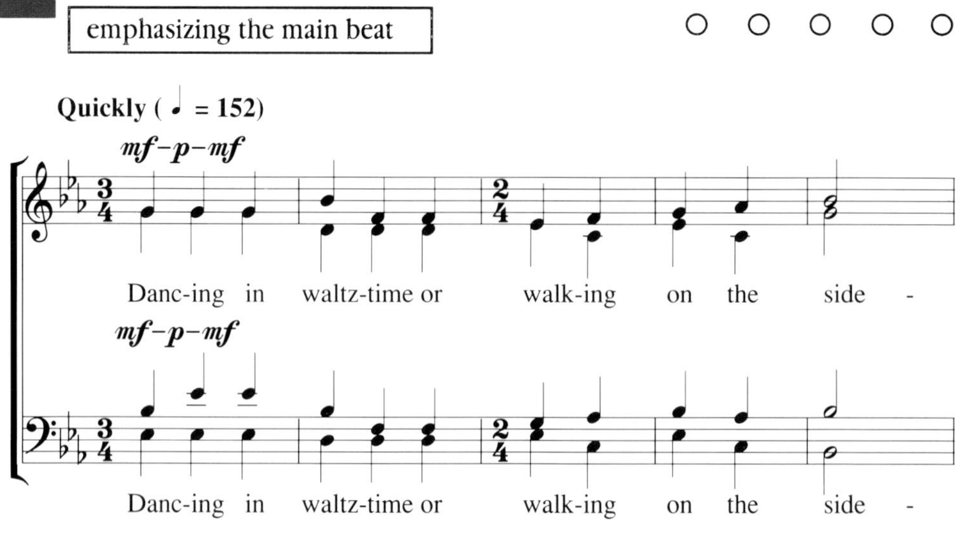

TIPS

A. Emphasize the first beat of each measure slightly.

B. Lighten the other beats.

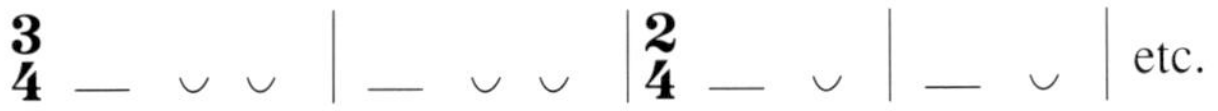

3/4 — ◡ ◡ | — ◡ ◡ | 2/4 — ◡ | — ◡ | etc.

12

cut-off on a rest

○ ○ ○ ○ ○

Quickly (♩ = 116)

Fought, hot, dot, bought;

Feed, lead, read, seed;

div.

Keep, deep, leap, beep; Sob. __________

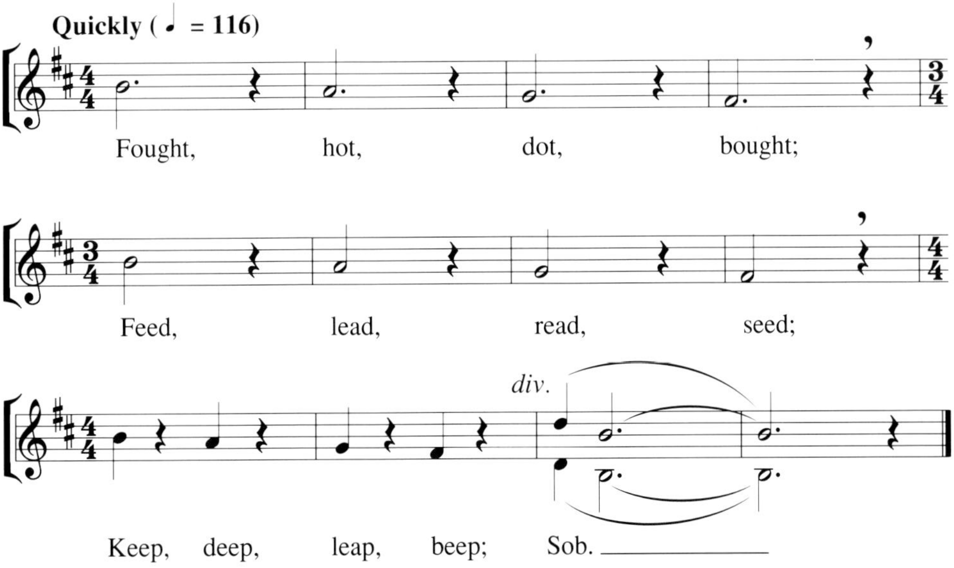

TIPS

A. Sing the final consonant of each word on the beat:

B. Feel the steady beat during each long note.

REMINDER **Drink plenty of water.**

13

ō

ō = long o
= a diphthong made from two sounds:

oh + u

(u = sounds like the "oo" in "moon")

Very quickly (♩. = 76)

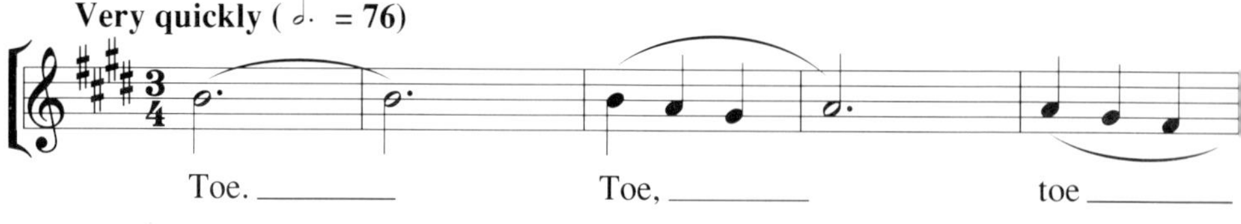

TIPS

A. The lips should form a circle for "oh." Let the teeth show slightly so that the lips do not muffle the clear "oh" sound.

B. Stretch out the "oh." Add the "u" at the last possible moment:

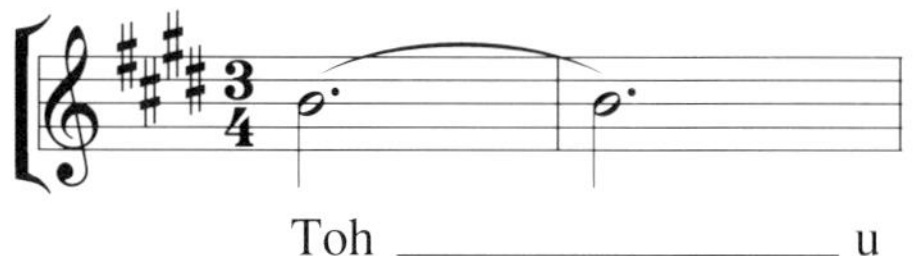

Sing the "u" lightly without emphasis.

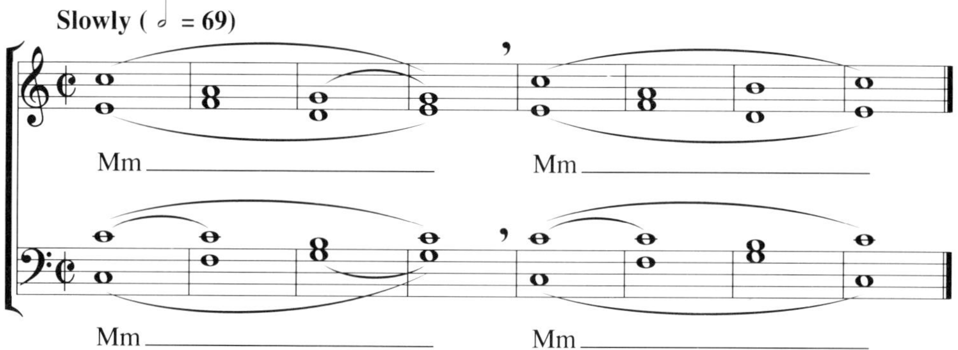

TIPS

A. Let the vibrations (resonance) of the "m" grow as you feel the support from the other pitches in the chord.

B. Start each morning with some humming to get your voice into shape.

15
tuning sustained notes

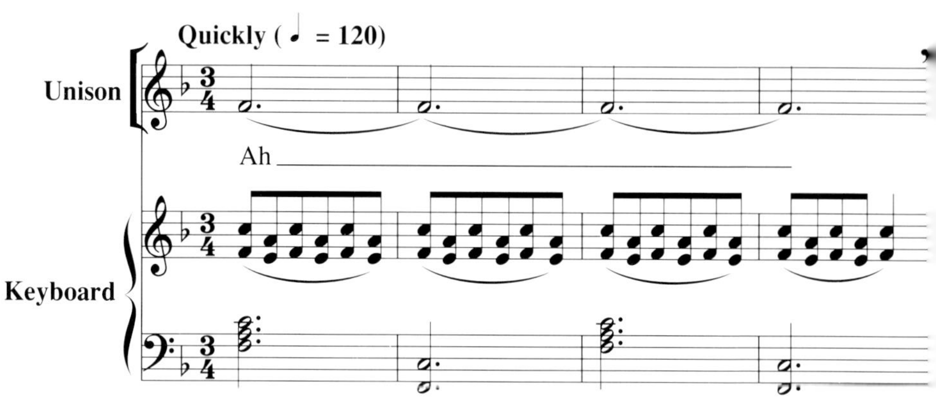
Quickly (♩ = 120)
Unison
Ah
Keyboard

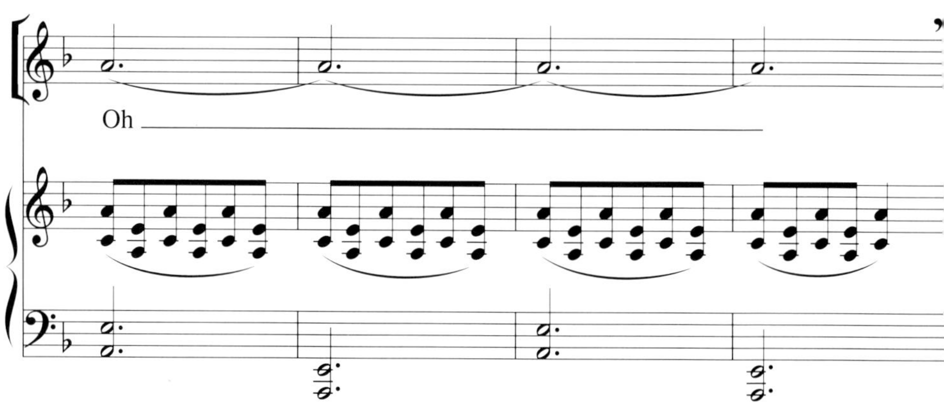
Oh

Ee

TIPS

A. Careful listening prevents out-of-tune singing. If the tuning goes out, automatically soften your voice to hear better.

B. If you are singing flat:

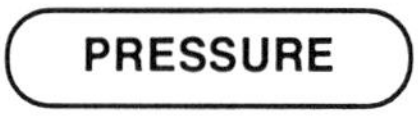

PRESSURE

Increase the air pressure in your tummy.

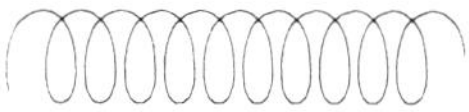

Keep the sound spinning through the air.

C. If you are singing sharp:

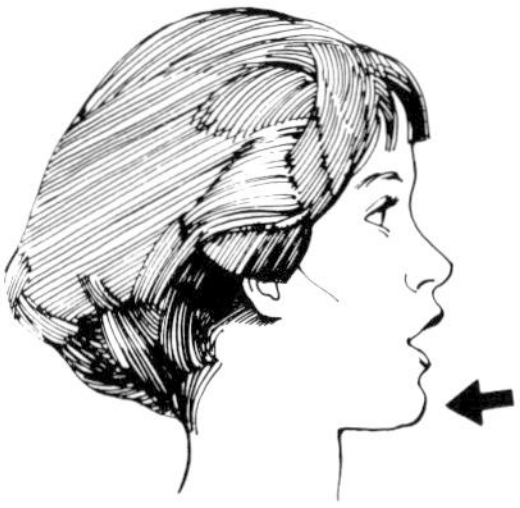

Keep your chin relaxed and back.

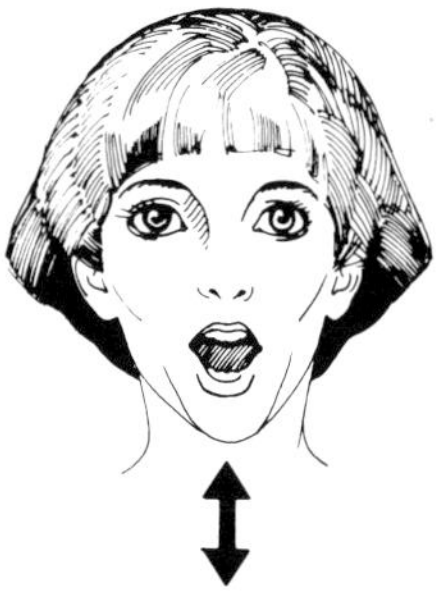

Let your jaw drop.

D.

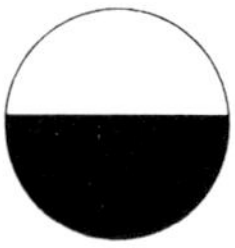

pitch too low = flat

pitch too high = sharp

in tune

brighten or relax vowels; ee oh

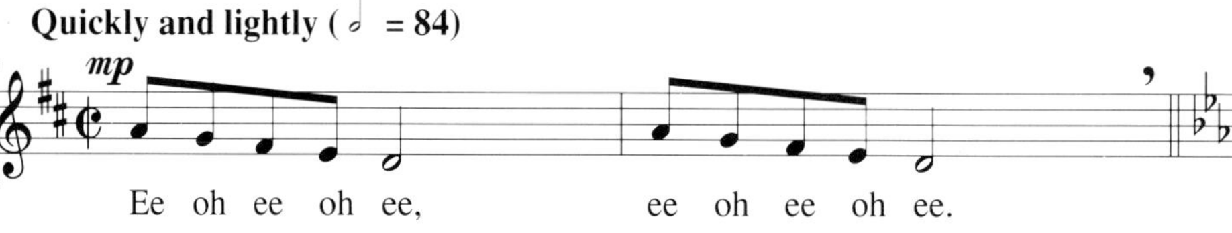

TIPS

A. Sing quickly and lightly, moving smoothly from vowel to vowel.

B. Move your mouth as little as possible. Let the "oh" take on some of the brightness of the "ee."

REMINDER **Drink plenty of water.**

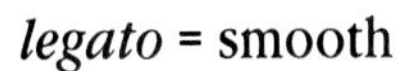

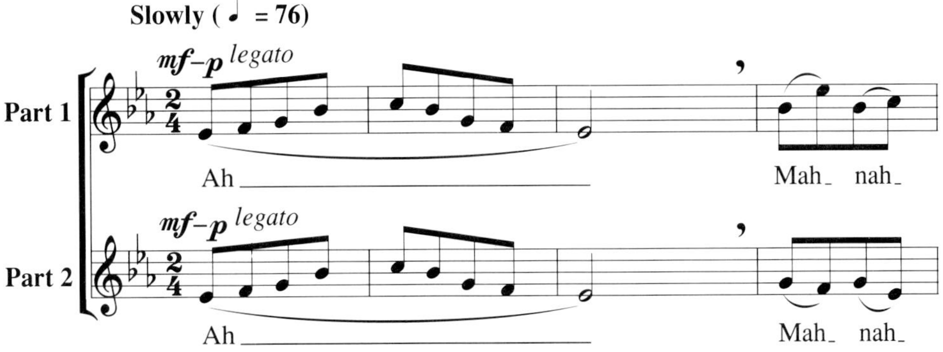

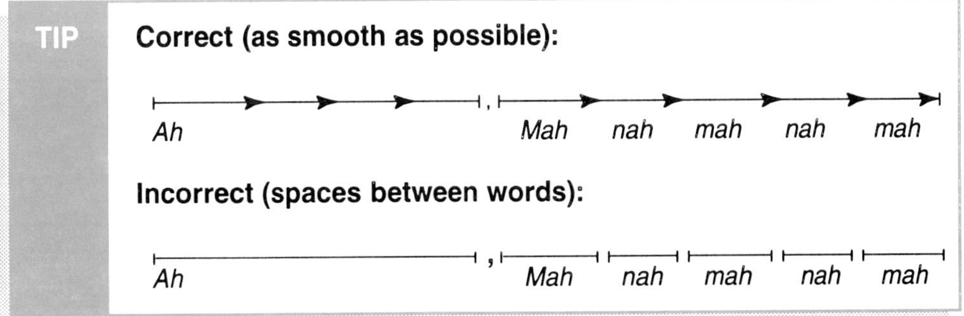

REMINDER Open your mouth north/south.

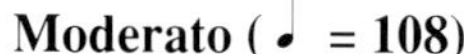

TIPS

A. **Stretch the spoken "f" and "s" for a whole beat.**

B. **When "f," "s" and "sh" occur in a word, make them very short, soft and exactly together with the other singers.**

C. **Sing each consonant at the same pitch as the vowel.**

19

"m" mask

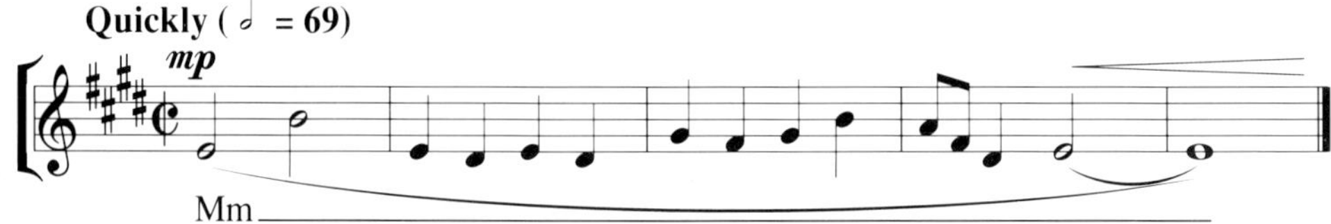

TIPS

A. Feel the vibrations (resonance) like a mask on your face.

B. *Crescendo* into a buzz at the end.

20

cut-off with no rest

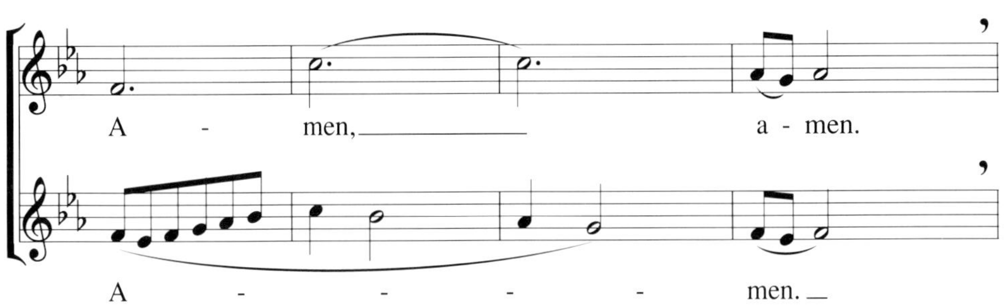

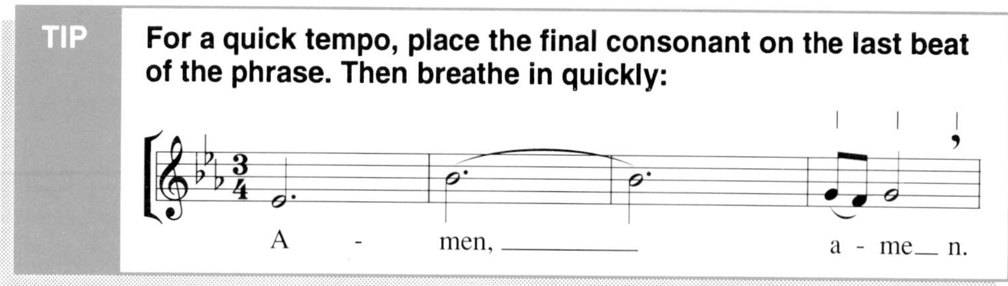
TIP
For a quick tempo, place the final consonant on the last beat of the phrase. Then breathe in quickly:
A - men,
a - me n.

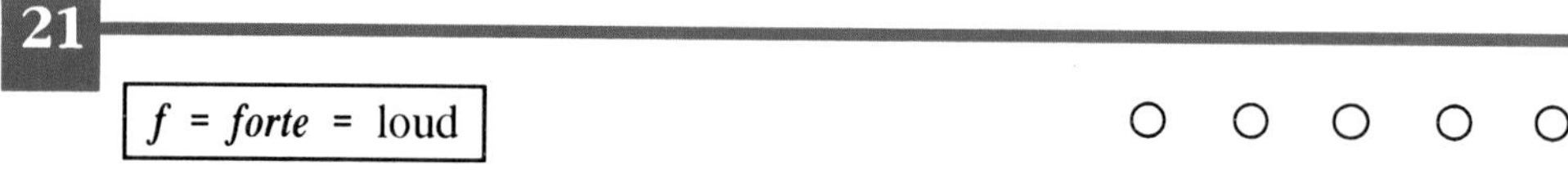
REMINDER
For an open throat, imagine the beginning of a yawn or a grapefruit in your throat.

21
f = forte = loud
Stately (♩ = 112)
of all this
His fa - ther was a lord of all this
His fa - ther was a lord of all this

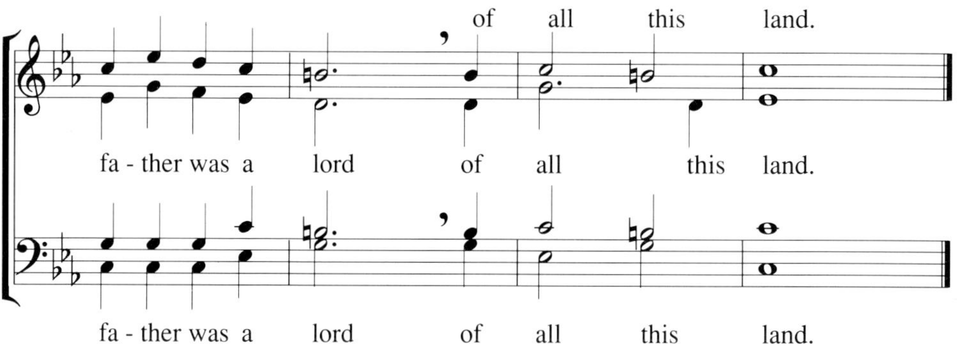

TIPS **For more volume with a quality sound:**

A. Support the air properly with more pressure from your tummy;

B. Open your mouth more;

C. Keep the tone forward;

D. Use the resonance in the "m" mask;

E. For extended *forte* passages in concert music, do not breathe too often.

22

phrases with different lengths

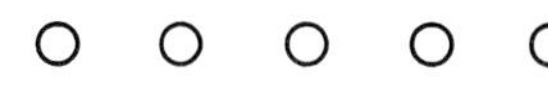

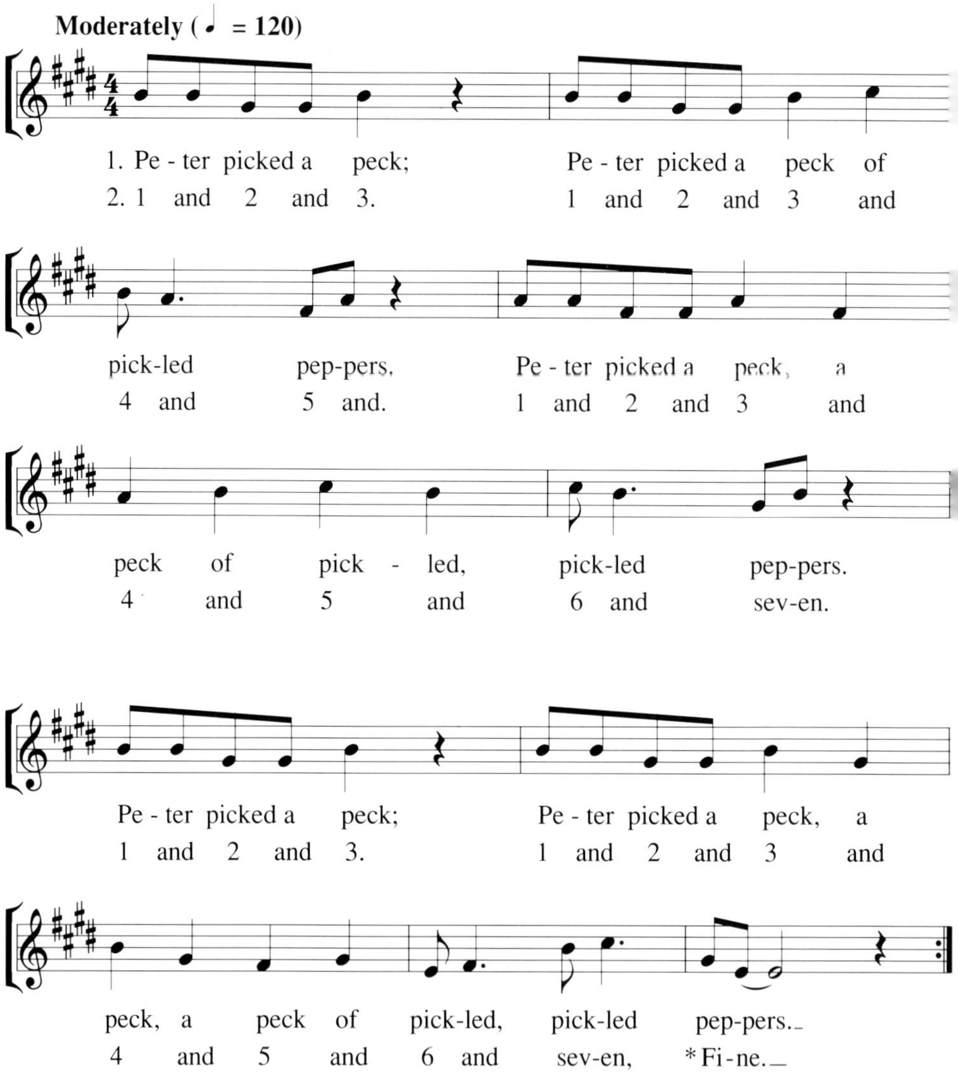

Moderately (♩ = 120)
1. Pe - ter picked a peck; Pe - ter picked a peck of
2. 1 and 2 and 3. 1 and 2 and 3 and
pick-led pep-pers. Pe - ter picked a peck, a
4 and 5 and. 1 and 2 and 3 and
peck of pick - led, pick-led pep-pers.
4 and 5 and 6 and sev-en.
Pe - ter picked a peck; Pe - ter picked a peck, a
1 and 2 and 3. 1 and 2 and 3 and
peck, a peck of pick-led, pick-led pep-pers.
4 and 5 and 6 and sev-en, *Fi-ne.

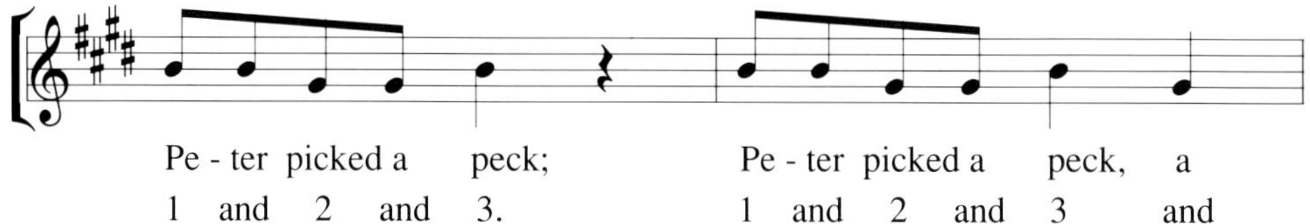

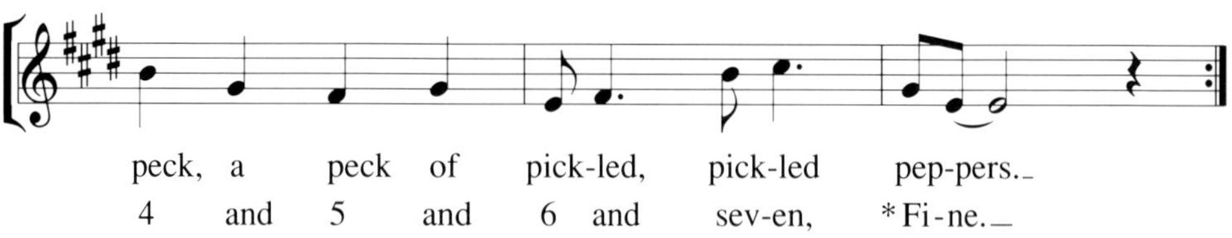

* Fine (pronounced <u>fee</u> - neh) = finished

TIPS

A. Look ahead in the music to pace yourself for the length of each phrase.

B. If the end of a phrase is weak, "lean into the phrase."

23

u

○ ○ ○ ○ ○

u = sounds like the "oo" in "moon"

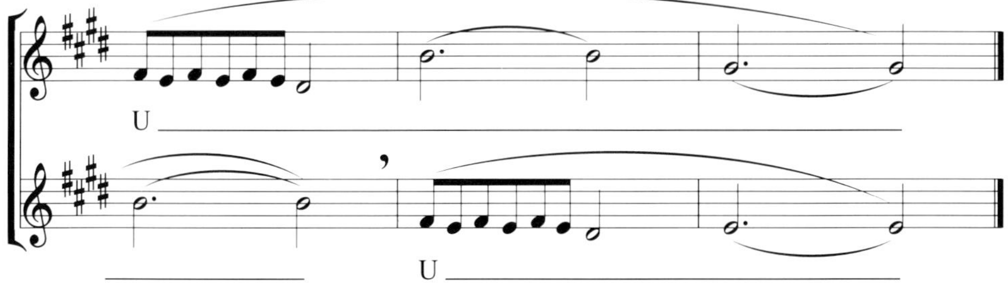

TIP Place the lips in a relaxed pucker.

REMINDER Breathe in the air until it fills up the back of your abdomen.

24

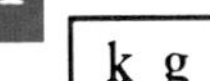

○ ○ ○ ○ ○

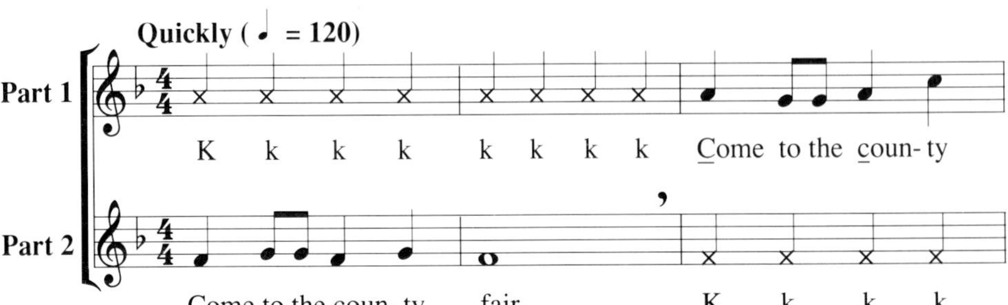

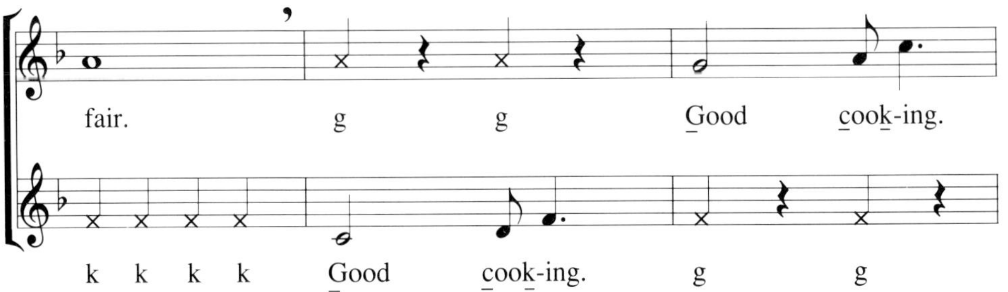

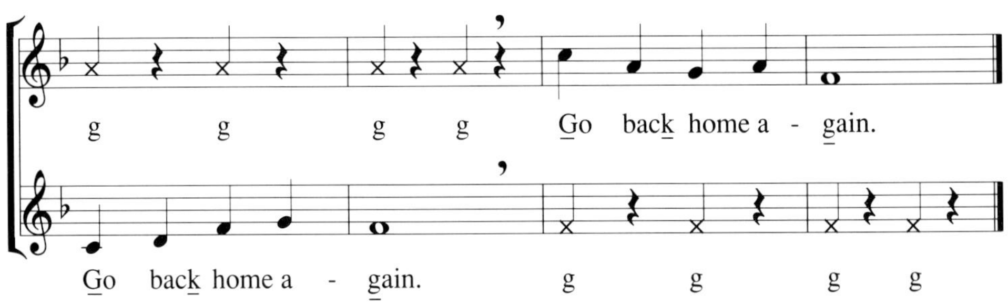

TIPS

A. For "k" and "g," make a tiny movement at the front of your mouth with your tongue.

B. Once your lips are in place, they should not move for the series of "k" or "g."

C. Make elephant ears (cup your hands behind your ears) to hear your own voice better.

25

balance for *forte*

TIPS

A. For a balanced choral sound, no voice or section should be louder than the rest of the choir.

B. Each singer is responsible for helping to maintain the balance. Listen carefully and consistently.

26

breathiness

Aggressively (♩ = 132)

TIPS

A. Make the "nyă" sound as nasty as possible to focus your voice.

B. Keep the resonance focused in your nose for singing the numbers.

REMINDER **Drink plenty of water.**

27

tuning when harmony changes in accompaniment

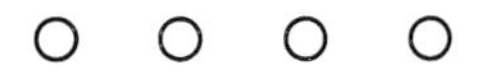

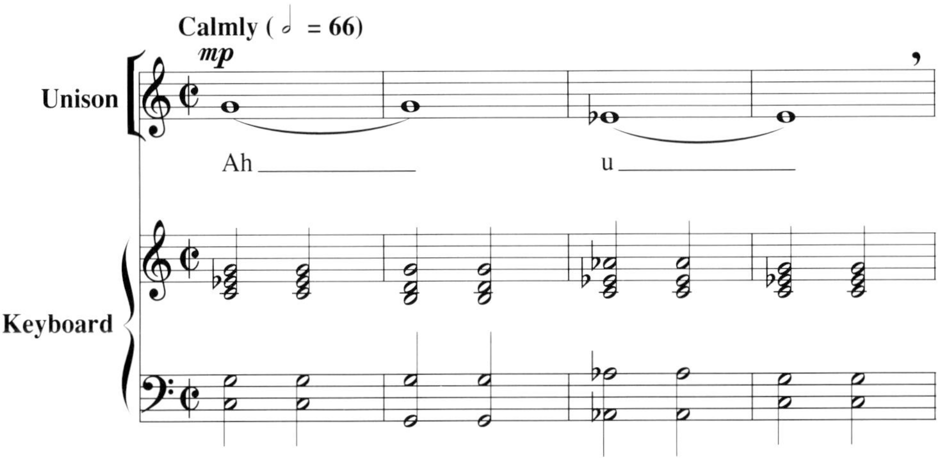

TIPS

A. Notes with the same pitch may sound a bit different with different chords; fit the pitch with the chord.

B. Listen to the bass part of the piano accompaniment. Balance your tuning with the bass part.

28

ā

○ ○ ○ ○ ○

ā = long a
= a diphthong made from two sounds:

eh + ee

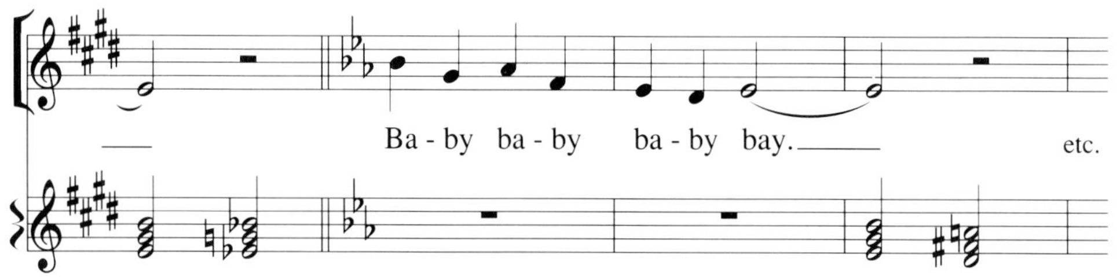

TIPS

A. Add the "ee" at the last possible moment. Sing the "ee" lightly without emphasis.

B. For ā , open your mouth north/south for more length.

REMINDER **Balance your body; keep your shoulders down.**

29

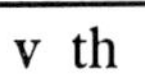

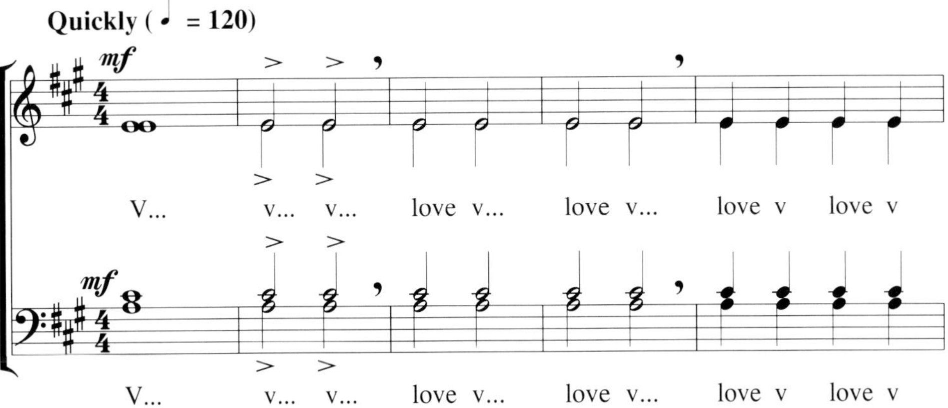

TIPS

A. **To increase the resonance, "motor" the sound for "v" and "th" like a toy car.**

B. **For "th," put your tongue between your teeth. "Th" may be voiced or unvoiced. For this warmup, use a voiced "th."**

REMINDER **Use a little bounce from the tummy for the accent.**

30

p = *piano* = soft

○ ○ ○ ○ ○

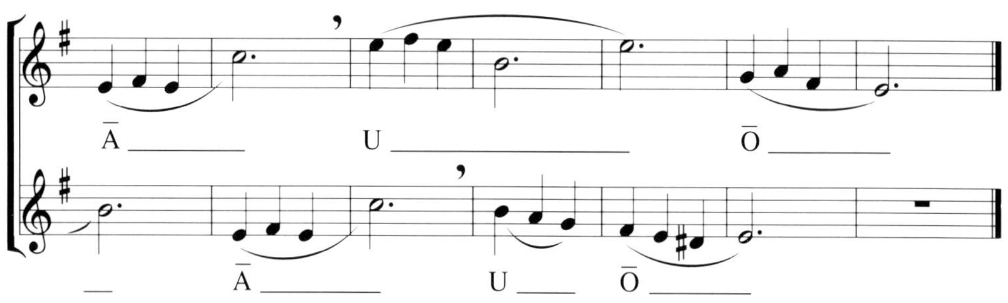

TIPS **For tuning difficulties in soft passages:**

- **A. Use good breath support;**
- **B. Listen carefully;**
- **C. Keep the energy in your voice;**
- **D. Keep the placement of the tone forward.**

31

long note in the middle of a phrase

○ ○ ○ ○ ○

TIPS

A. **Spin the sound forward on the long note in mid-phrase.**

B. **Add some momentum at the end of the long note as it moves into the next note.**

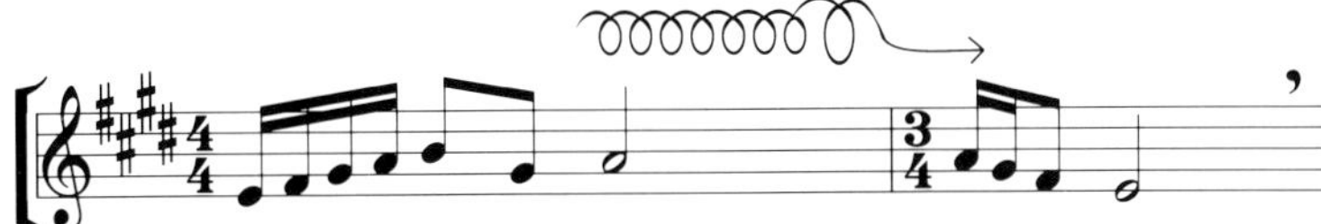

C. **For a cut-off on a vowel, simply keep the vowel spinning until you breathe in on the beat. Do not close your mouth for the cut-off.**

32

cresc. = *crescendo* = gradually louder =

○ ○ ○ ○ ○

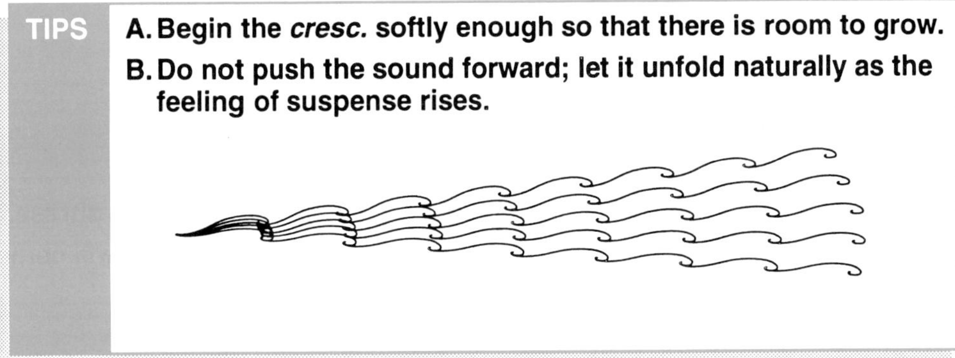

REMINDER

For an open throat, imagine the beginning of a yawn or a grapefruit in your throat.

33

cut-off on a half beat

⅃ = 1/2 = cut off on the half beat

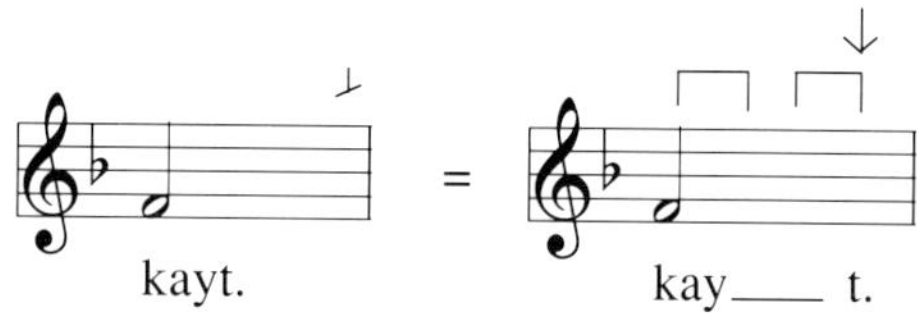

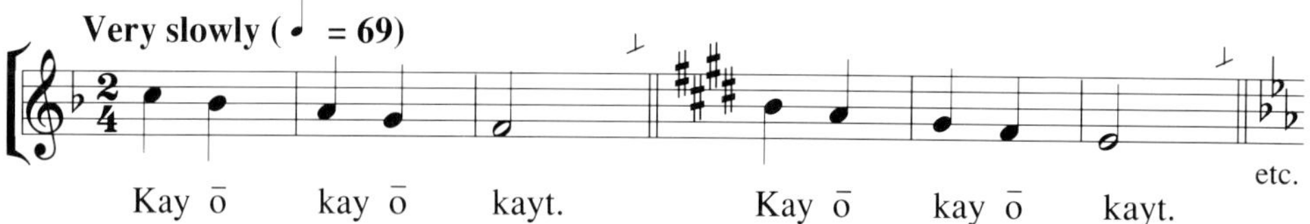

TIPS

A. Feel the eighth note pulses on the last note of each phrase.

B. For the cut-off, the second vowel of the diphthong will come right before the final consonant:

Sing the "ee" lightly without emphasis.

REMINDER **Drink plenty of water.**

34

th h ch

(♩ = 104 - 116)

TIPS

A. Use an unvoiced "th" for this warmup. Move the tongue quickly between the teeth like a snake tongue.

B. For a diphthong on a cut-off, place the final vowel of the diphthong briefly on the rest. Do not emphasize the final vowel.

Vowel on Rest: throh__ u

Consonant on Rest: thank hi__ m

C. Speaking is usually harder on the voice than singing. Avoid situations which are stressful to the voice:

- **Loud talking (particularly on buses);**
- **Yelling;**
- **Screaming;**
- **Clearing your throat.**

35

tuning with the harmony of the choir

○ ○ ○ ○ ○

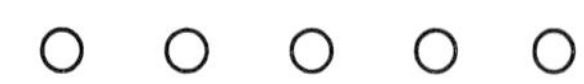

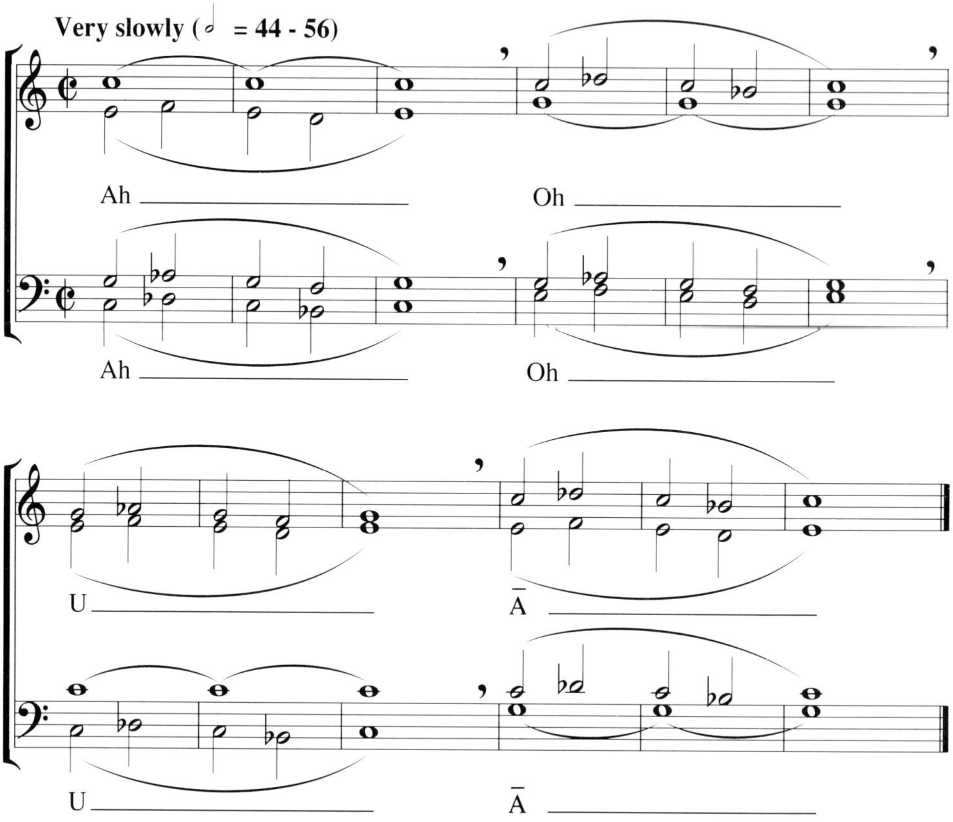
Very slowly (𝅗𝅥 = 44 - 56)
Ah
Oh
Ah
Oh
U
Ā
U
Ā

TIPS	
	A. Tune in quickly when the pitch changes.
	B. When the pitch remains the same, keep the tone simmering (alive) for level tuning.

REMINDER **Breathe in the air until it fills up your lower back.**

36

resonance with "z"

TIPS

A. Exaggerate the "z" to get the vibrations buzzing.

Dizzzy izzzy day ——

B. Place your hands loosely on your face with your fingers touching your cheekbones and your palms touching your jaw to feel the resonance better:

C. Let the "d" throw the vocal placement forward.

D. Open your mouth quickly for "ay."

37

tuning and projecting a humming sound

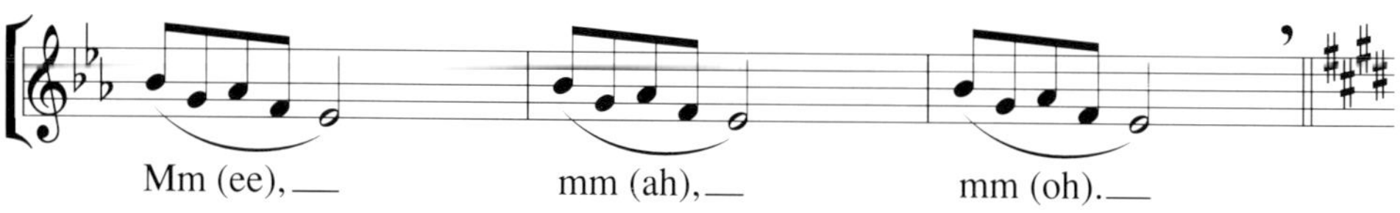

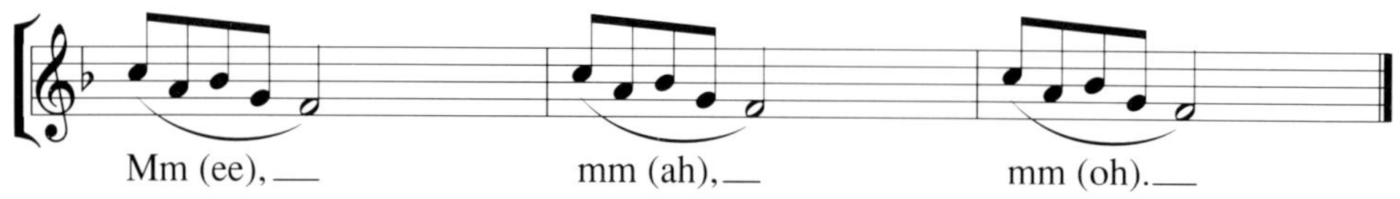

TIP **"mm(ee)" = hum "m" but shape an "ee" inside the mouth**

FIRST YEAR PROGRESS CHART

CIRCLE the appropriate number:

1 - understands the skill	4 - good progress
2 - can do the skill	5 - excellent progress
3 - some improvement shown	6 - remembers consistently

Singers in Position - balanced	1 2 3 4 5 6
1a. building tummy muscles	1 2 3 4 5 6
1b. b p ; working the lips	1 2 3 4 5 6
1c. short consonants; long vowels	1 2 3 4 5 6
- vowel on the beat	1 2 3 4 5 6
1d. ah: tone quality	1 2 3 4 5 6
1e. open mouth	1 2 3 4 5 6
2. building endurance for breath	1 2 3 4 5 6
- expand tummy	1 2 3 4 5 6
- shoulders down	1 2 3 4 5 6
Singers in Position - hold book correctly	1 2 3 4 5 6
3. d t j ; working the tongue	1 2 3 4 5 6
4. breathing early in rhythm	1 2 3 4 5 6
Singers in Position - sit hard on bones	1 2 3 4 5 6
- feet flat on the floor	1 2 3 4 5 6
- your back away from chair	1 2 3 4 5 6
5. steady beat - no toe tapping	1 2 3 4 5 6
Breathing - to the lower back	1 2 3 4 5 6
- shoulders down	1 2 3 4 5 6
6. tuning repeated pitches	1 2 3 4 5 6
7. ee	1 2 3 4 5 6
8. m ; voice placed forward	1 2 3 4 5 6
9. l n	1 2 3 4 5 6
10. open throat	1 2 3 4 5 6
Quick check: Drinking water?	1 2 3 4 5 6
11. emphasizing the main beat (where appropriate)	1 2 3 4 5 6
12. cut-off on rest	1 2 3 4 5 6
13. long o	1 2 3 4 5 6
14. “m” hum	1 2 3 4 5 6

Item	Rating
15. tuning sustained notes - sing softly	1 2 3 4 5 6
- flat: increase pressure, keep sound spinning	1 2 3 4 5 6
- sharp: keep chin relaxed and back; drop jaw	1 2 3 4 5 6
16. brighten or relax vowels: ee oh	1 2 3 4 5 6
17. *legato*	1 2 3 4 5 6
18. f s sh	1 2 3 4 5 6
19. "m" mask	1 2 3 4 5 6
20. cut-off with no rest	1 2 3 4 5 6
Quick check: Posture?	1 2 3 4 5 6
21. *forte* - breath support	1 2 3 4 5 6
- open mouth	1 2 3 4 5 6
- forward tone	1 2 3 4 5 6
- resonance	1 2 3 4 5 6
22. phrases with different lengths - look ahead	1 2 3 4 5 6
- lean into the phrase	1 2 3 4 5 6
23. u	1 2 3 4 5 6
24. k g	1 2 3 4 5 6
25. balance for *forte*	1 2 3 4 5 6
26. breathiness	1 2 3 4 5 6
27. tuning with bass of accompaniment	1 2 3 4 5 6
28. long a	1 2 3 4 5 6
29. v th	1 2 3 4 5 6
30. *piano*: tuning - breath support	1 2 3 4 5 6
- listen	1 2 3 4 5 6
- energy	1 2 3 4 5 6
- forward tone	1 2 3 4 5 6
Quick check: Breathing?	1 2 3 4 5 6
31. long note in mid-phrase	1 2 3 4 5 6
32. *cresc.*	1 2 3 4 5 6
33. cut-off on a half beat	1 2 3 4 5 6
34. th h ch	1 2 3 4 5 6
35. tuning harmony with the choir - tuning quickly	1 2 3 4 5 6
- simmer tone for level tuning	1 2 3 4 5 6
36. resonance with "z"	1 2 3 4 5 6
37. tuning and projecting "m"	1 2 3 4 5 6
◆ ◆ **CONGRATULATIONS!** ◆ ◆	

Second Year

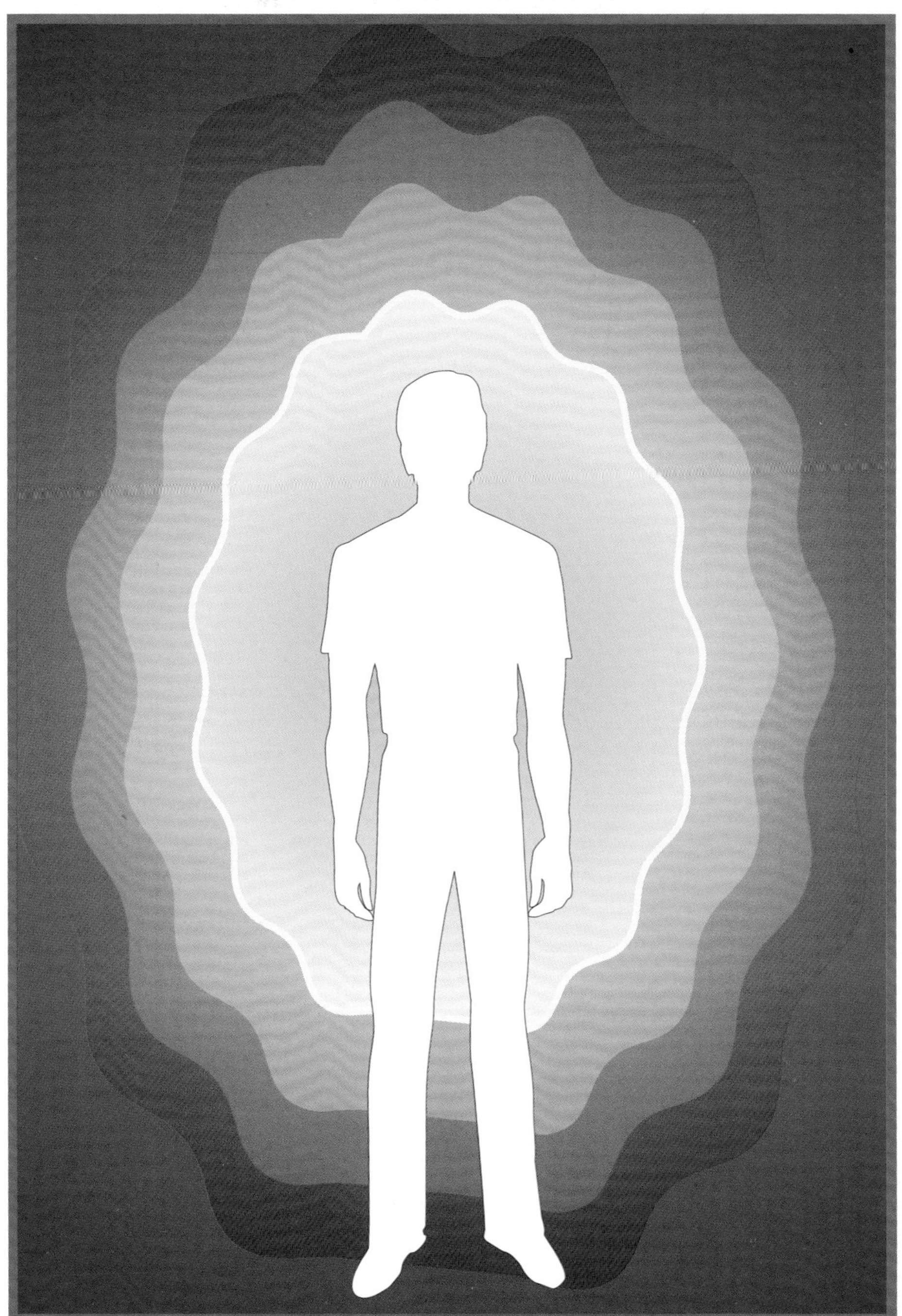

When you use your whole body to sing, the sound seems to come from the depths of the soul.

SINGERS IN POSITION

When you sing, think of your body as a tree.
Your body is tall and strong.

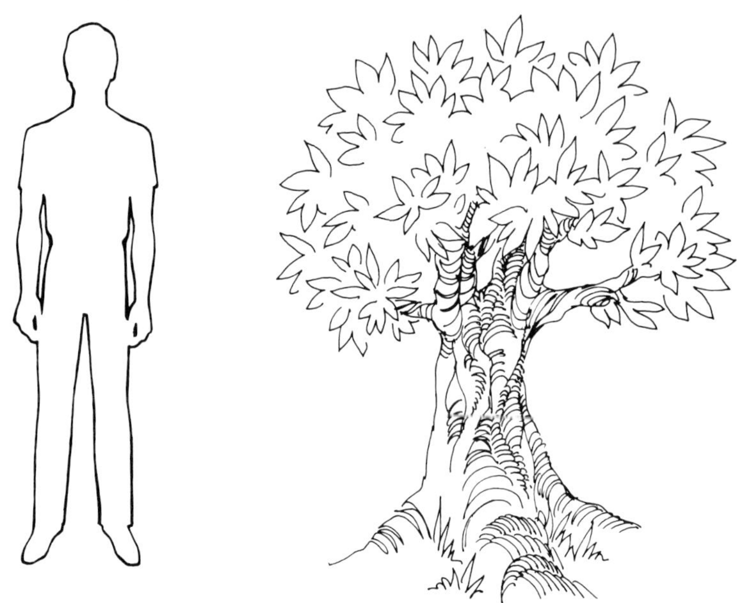

♦ Your feet are rooted to the ground. Feel the strength flowing from the ground upward through your body. Breathe in through the roots.

♦ A tree is flexible enough to move a bit with the wind. Keep your knees slightly flexed so that your body remains relaxed and flexible.

Use the strength of your full body to sing.

38

drop the jaw

○ ○ ○ ○ ○

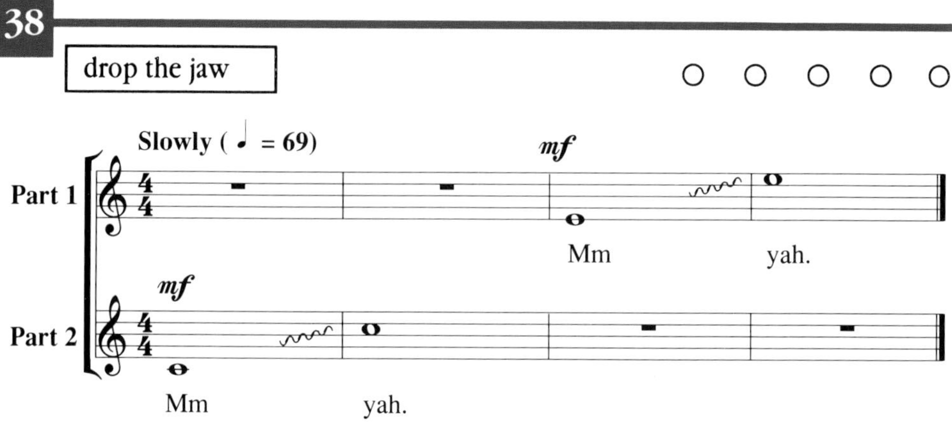

TIPS

A. Let the "m" vibrate like a motor getting ready to quick-start for a race.

B. During the last part of the fourth beat, glide up quickly to the top pitch. Do not sing each scale pitch separately; let the voice slide through all the pitches "between the cracks."

C. Feel the gravity as the jaw drops way down during the glide. Do not force the jaw down.

39

rhythmic diction

○ ○ ○ ○ ○

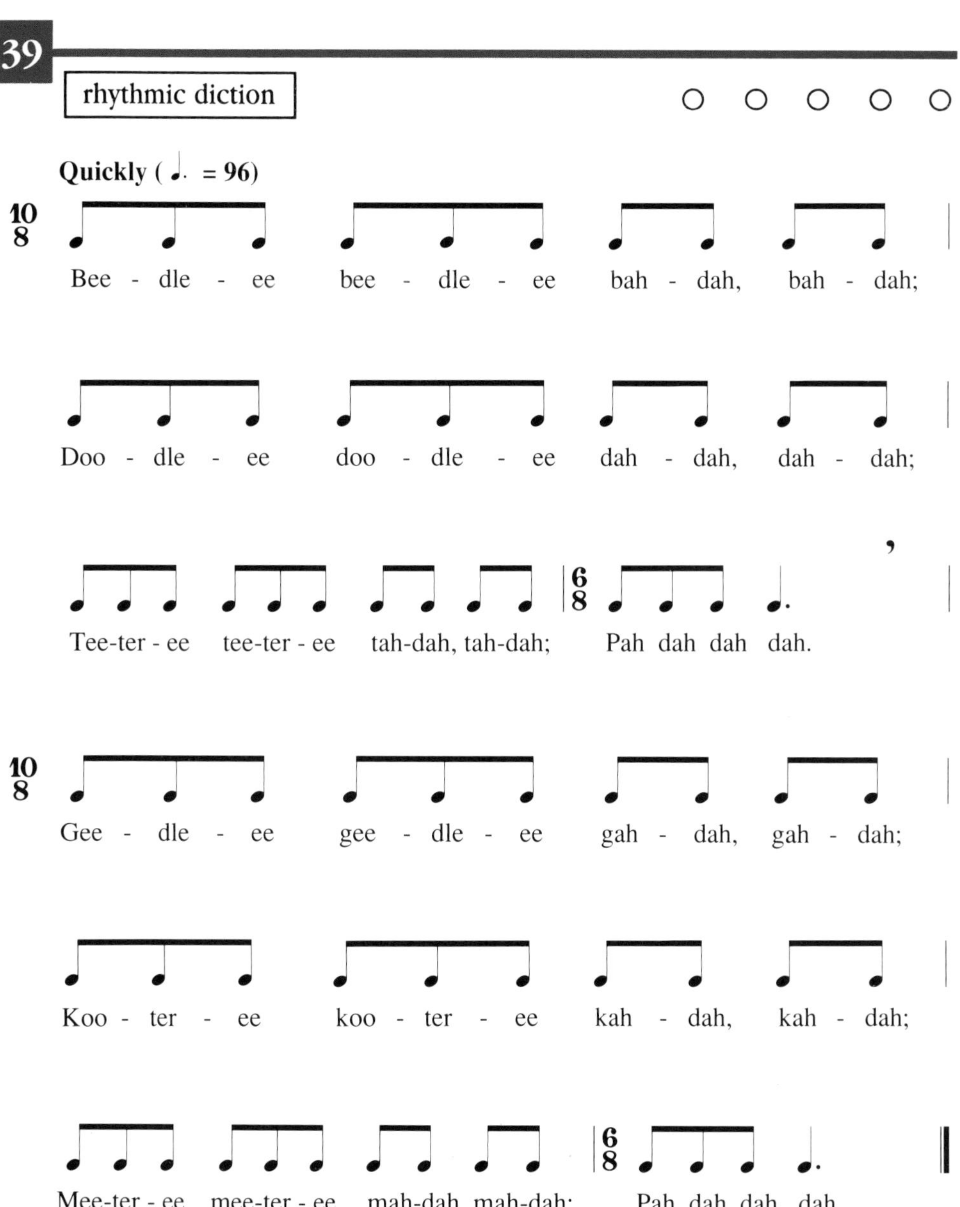

TIPS

A. When you form the consonants at the front of your mouth, you can:

- ♦ **Move through each consonant quickly;**
- ♦ **Keep your voice placement forward;**
- ♦ **Make the lyrics easier to understand.**

Inefficient consonants can waste a lot of energy.

B. Place a slight emphasis on the first eighth note in each grouping:

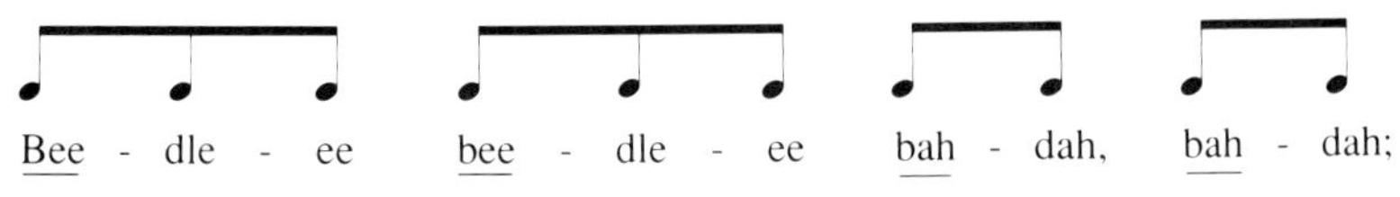

REMINDER

Start each morning with some humming to get your voice in shape.

40

bl cl gl fl pl sl

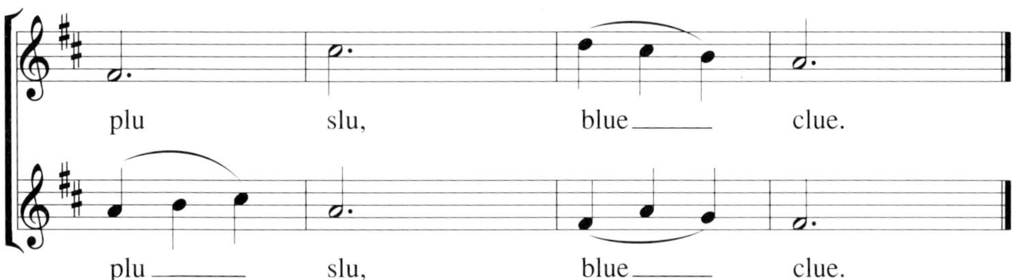

TIPS

A. Sing quickly through the "l":

blu **not** *ballu*

Start the vowel on the beat; place the consonants right before the beat.

B. Sing the warmup in one breath. Think of the phrasing as you sing:

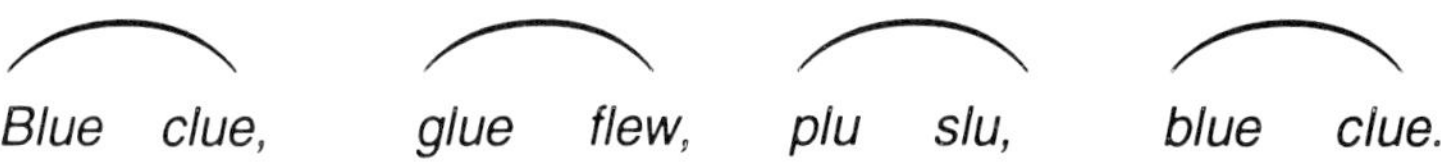

Blue clue, glue flew, plu slu, blue clue.

This exercise uses short fragments joined together to make one phrase.

REMINDER **For a healthy voice, drink plenty of water each day.**

41

TIPS

A. Exaggerate the "m."

B. Let the resonance of the "m" move quickly into the vowel sound.

C. Notice which vowel is your best sounding vowel. Concentrate on improving each of the other vowels.

D. If you have difficulty hearing the true sound of your own voice, try singing into a corner. Listen to the reflection of sound.

Use a corner with no curtains or wall hangings to mute the sound.

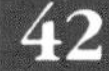

42

gliding in mid-range

○ ○ ○ ○ ○

Slowly (♩ = 72)
mp
Ah, ______
ah, ______
etc.

TIPS

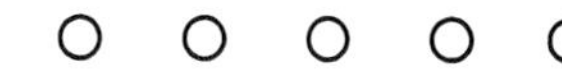

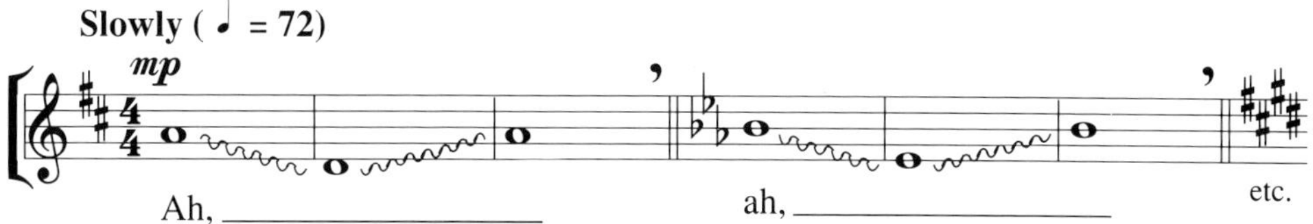

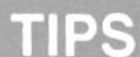

A. Glide very slowly to the next pitch. Start the pitch moving on the first beat; take four full beats to get to the next pitch.

B. Smooth out the sound in the areas where your voice tends to "skip" rather than move in a continuous glide.

not

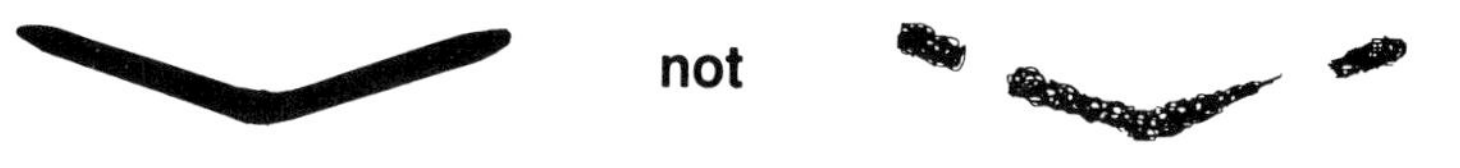

43

slurs

○ ○ ○ ○ ○

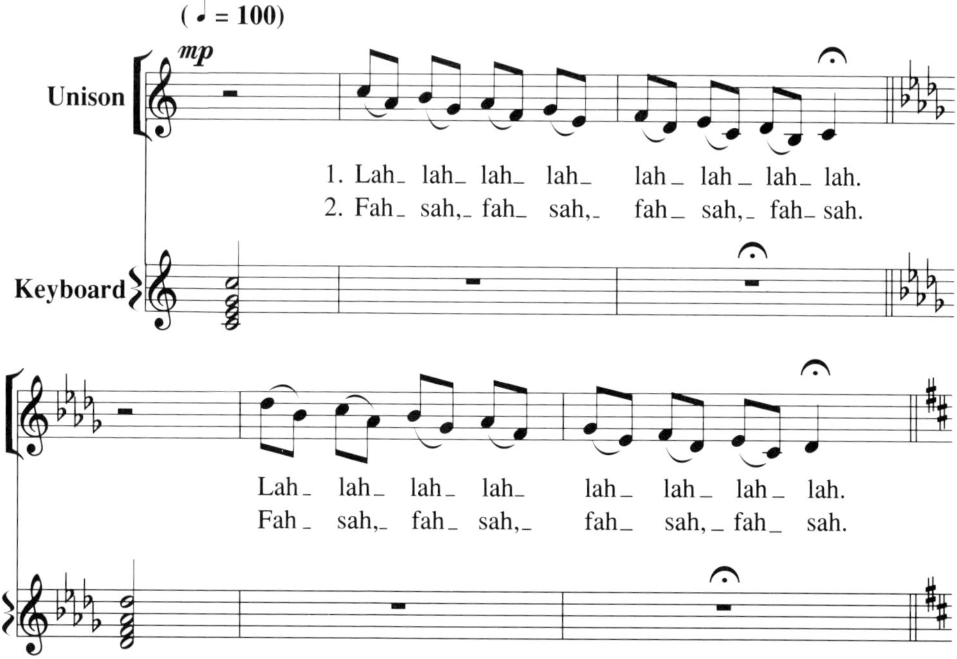

(♩ = 100)
mp
Unison
1. Lah_ lah_ lah_ lah_ lah_ lah_ lah_ lah.
2. Fah_ sah,_ fah_ sah,_ fah_ sah,_ fah_ sah.
Keyboard
Lah_ lah_ lah_ lah_ lah_ lah_ lah_ lah.
Fah_ sah,_ fah_ sah,_ fah_ sah,_ fah_ sah.

TIPS

A. Raise your ribcage as you breathe in. Keep the ribcage up as you sing. (When you are not singing, relax your ribcage.)

B. Just before you begin each phrase, imagine the first pitch in the top of your head so that you begin singing at the higher pitch level:

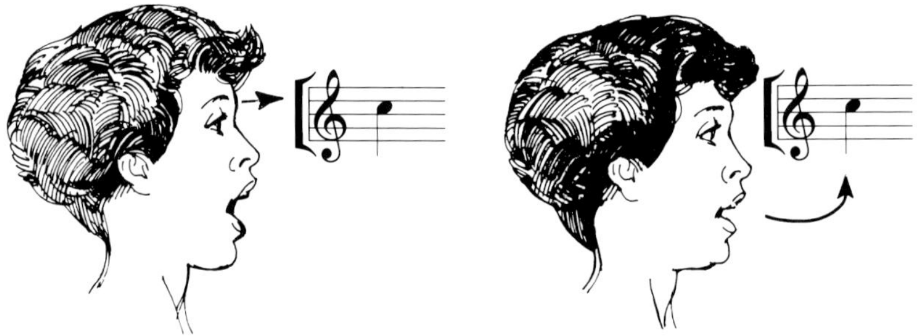

Think the pitch.

Do not reach up to the pitch.

C. Think of each slur as one unit of sound rather than two separate notes.

D. Sing the low pitches lightly. Use a smaller circle of sound to lighten the tone for the entire phrase.

REMINDER

Think of your body as a tree. Use the strength of your full body to sing.

44

changing tempo suddenly

Slowly

1. We reach to - ward the__ fu - ture.
2. Each mo - ment is an e - ter-ni - ty.

Quickly

Blue light sur - rounds us in a cir - cle.

Heart - beat goes tick - ing fast - er, fast - er.

Time is be - gin - ning to ac - cel - er - ate.

Slowly

Hold stead-y.__

TIP Prepare yourself in the measure before each tempo change.

45

sp sk st squ

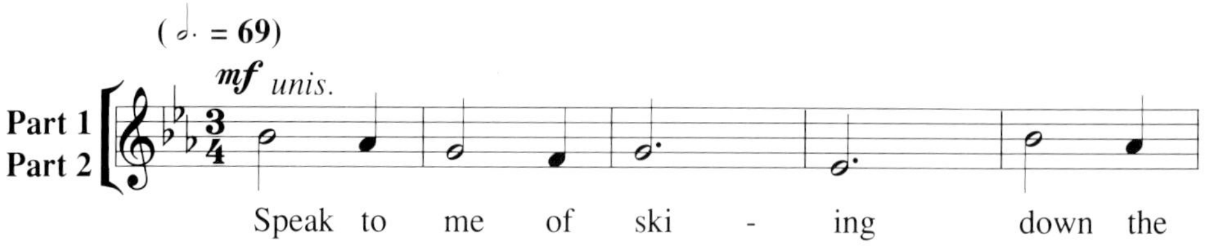

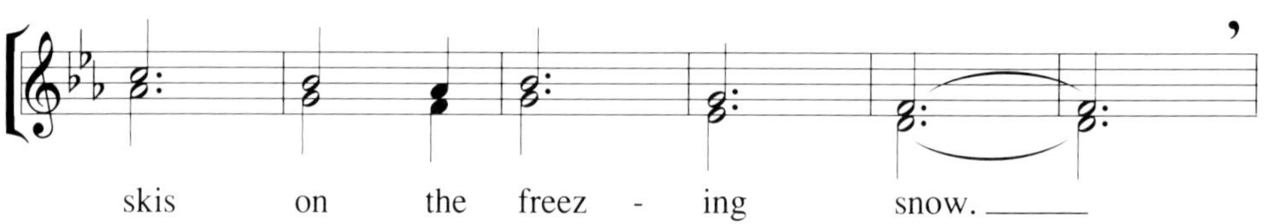

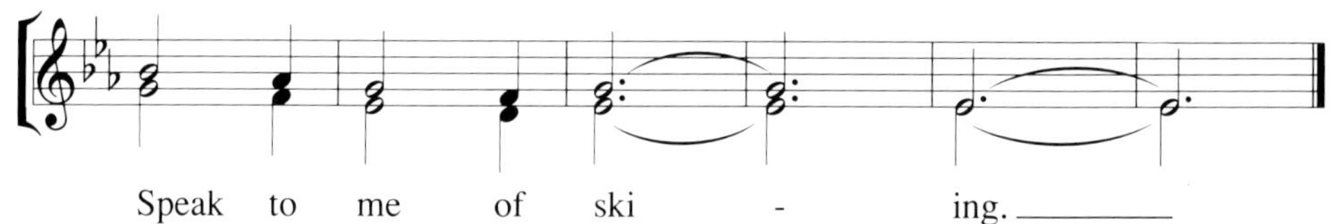

TIPS

A. Keep each "s" as short as possible. Concentrate on enunciating the following consonant.

B. Your diction will improve when you think of the meaning of the words as you sing.

music = communication

46

tuning a melody with framework pitches

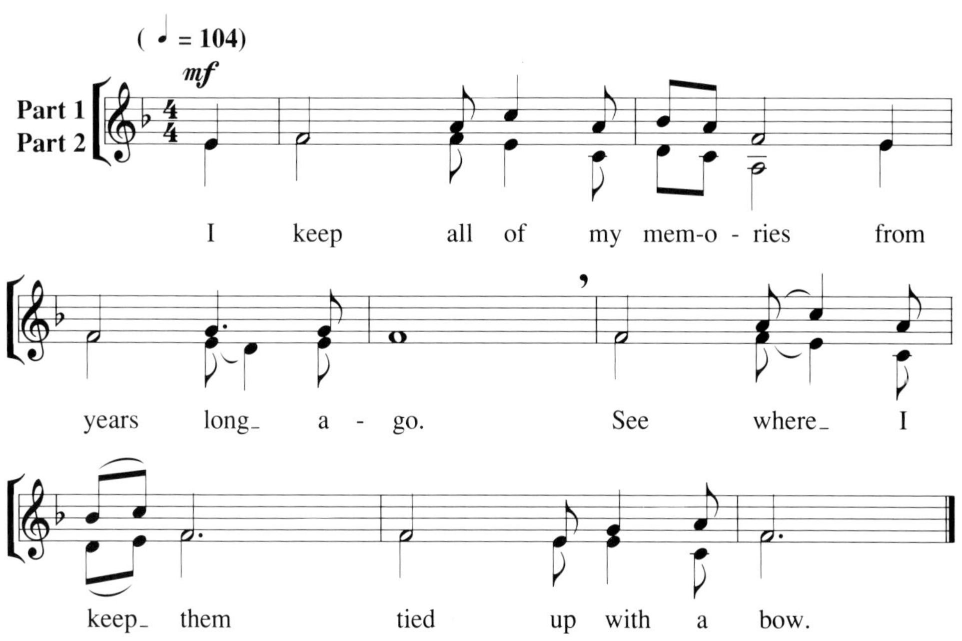

TIP

Framework pitches:

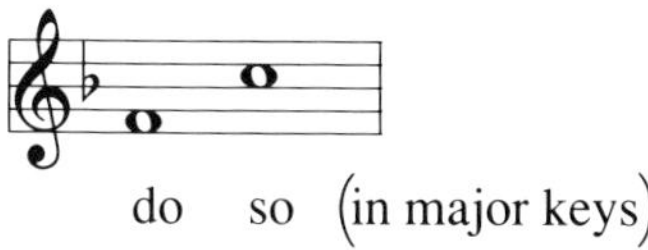

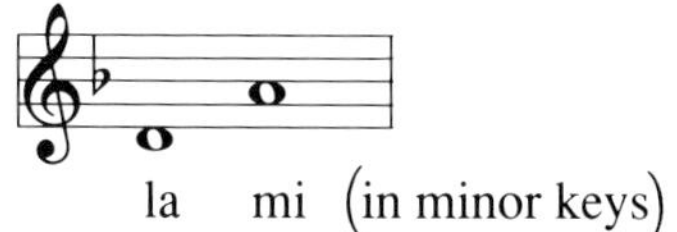

When the melody returns to the same framework pitch, make sure that the pitch is still in tune. Each F must sound at exactly the same pitch.

REMINDER

Avoid yelling, screaming and loud talking (particularly on buses).

47

short "a"

TIPS

A. Short "a" sounds like the "a" in "cat."

B. Sing very lightly for short vowels.

REMINDER

Start each morning with some humming to get your voice in shape.

48

extending your range up

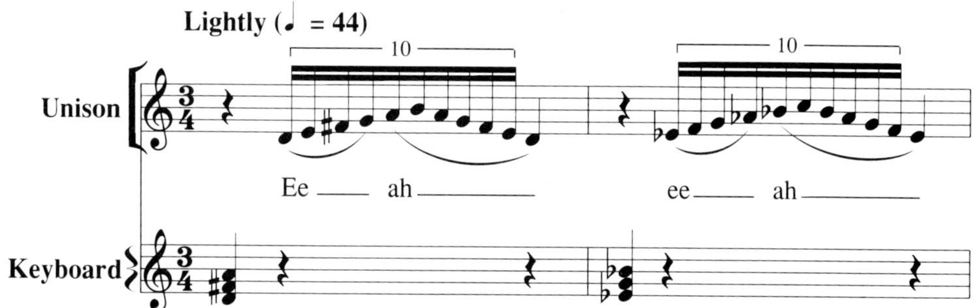

TIPS

A. Move quickly and lightly through the pitches. A "taste" of high pitches stretches the range much better than longer durations.

B. As the pitches get higher, drop the jaw more. Do not point your head up as the pitch ascends.

C. Feel your throat expand when you move into the "ah."

D. Use the momentum of the phrase to lift the "ah" over the top and down again:

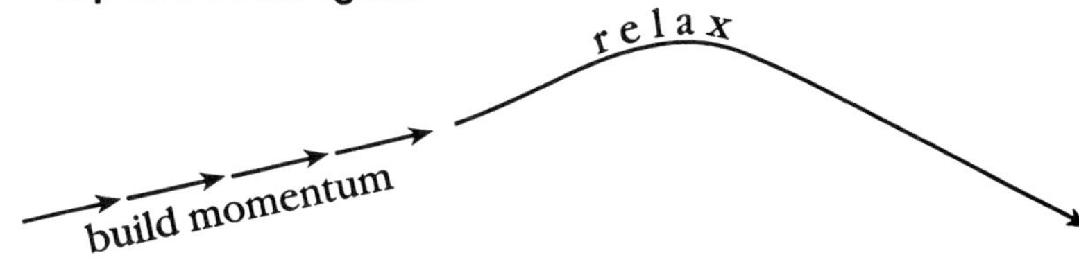

49

syncopation

Lightly (♩ = 132)

mf

Part 1

Dah dah dah dah_ dah dah, Dah dah dah dah_ dah dah,

mf

Part 2
Part 3

Dah dah_ Dah dah_

Dah dah dah dah_ dah dah, dah dah dah dah._

Dah dah_ Dah dah._

TIPS

A. Leave no space between the notes. A space interrupts the rhythm.

B. Do not move your tongue too much. A quick, thin tongue movement creates a precise, percussive sound; a larger movement is too sluggish.

w wh

○ ○ ○ ○ ○

1. Wee wee wee wee, weh weh weh weh, wah wah wah wah, woh woh woh woh,
2. Whee wee wee wee, wheh weh weh weh, whah wah wah wah, whoh woh woh woh,

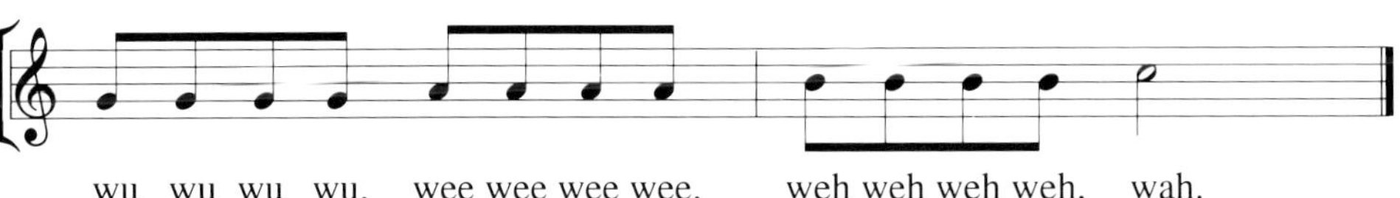

wu wu wu wu, wee wee wee wee, weh weh weh weh, wah.
whu wu wu wu, whee wee wee wee, wheh weh weh weh, whah.

TIPS

A. The lips do a glide to form "w." Go through the glide quickly.

B. To make "wh" clearer, you may wish to use the English pronunciation:

wh = hw

C. Practice singing words beginning with "w" to sustained notes if you need to make your vowels rounder.

REMINDER **For a healthy voice, drink plenty of water each day.**

51

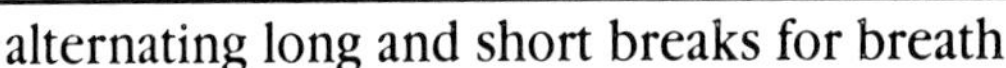

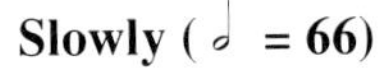

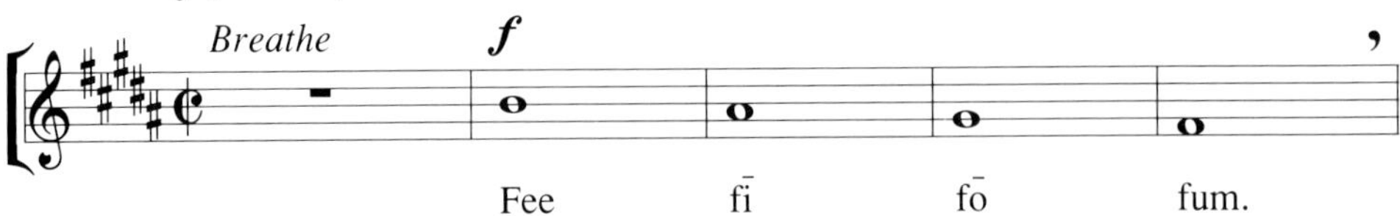

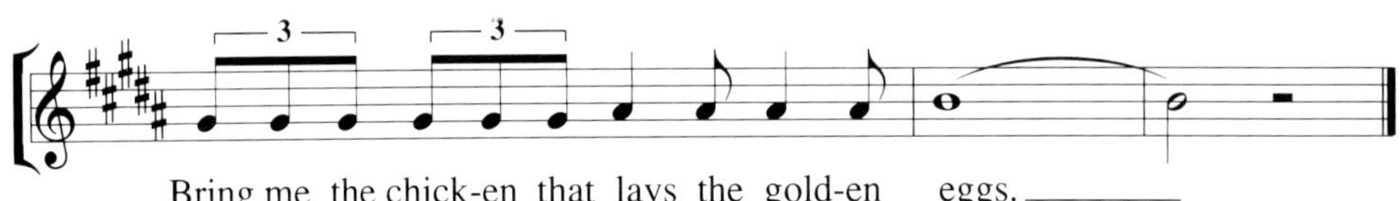

TIPS

A. For long breaths, breathe the air in through the soles of your feet.

B. For short breaths, breathe in quickly from the tummy.

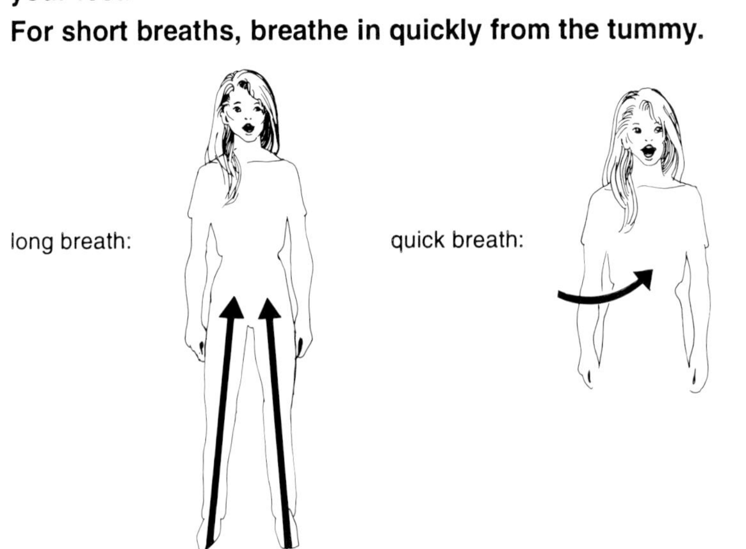

REMINDER **Balance your body; keep your shoulders down.**

52

oy

○ ○ ○ ○ ○

oy = a diphthong made from two sounds:

oh + ee

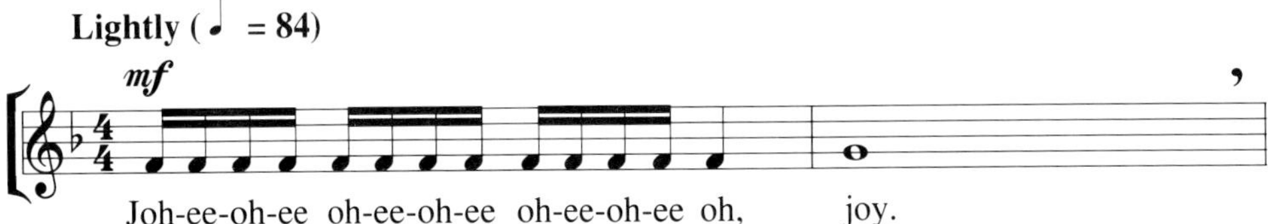

TIPS

A. Move the mouth as little as possible as you move lightly back and forth from "oh" to "ee."

B. For "joy," stretch out the first vowel; add the second vowel just for a fraction of a second on the fourth beat of the measure before you breathe in:

| | | |

joh ______________ ee

Sing the second vowel lightly without emphasis.

53

terraced dynamics

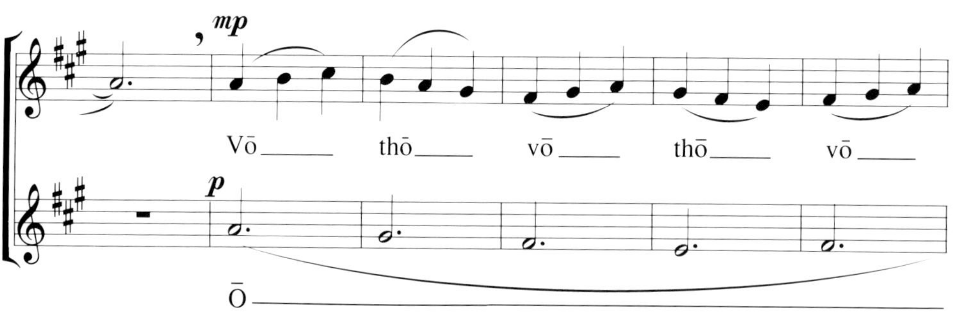

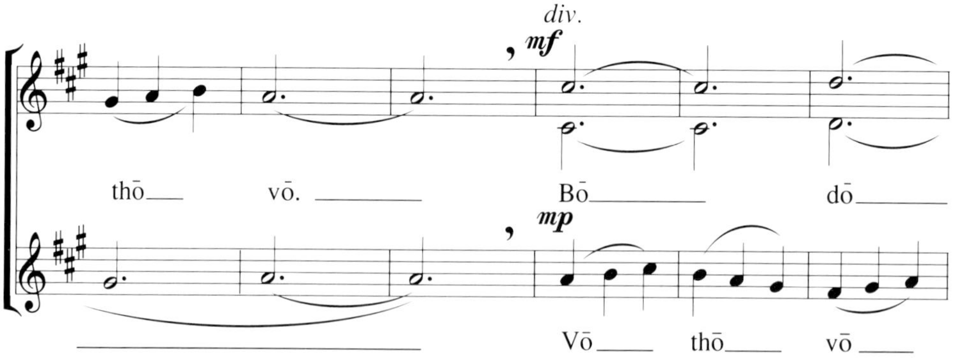

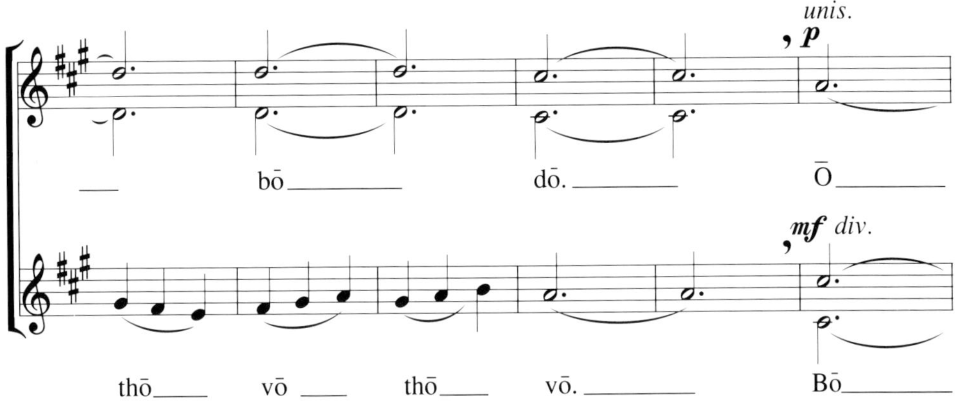

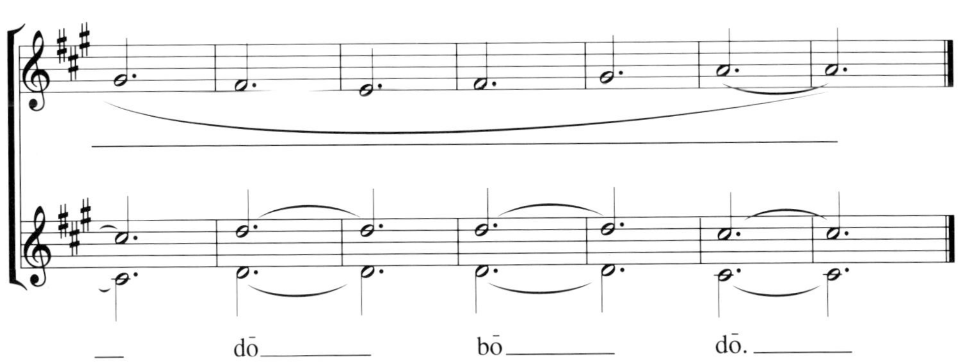

TIPS

A. Think of each dynamic marking as being at a different level of sound:

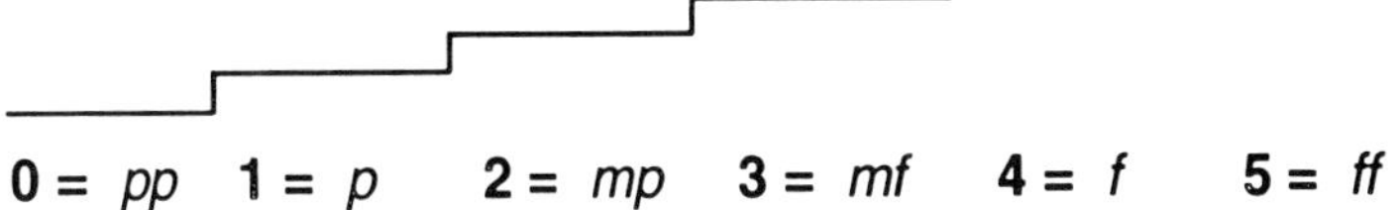

0 = *pp* 1 = *p* 2 = *mp* 3 = *mf* 4 = *f* 5 = *ff*

B. Sing at the dynamic level marked even though another vocal part may have a different marking.

REMINDER

Think of your body as a tree. Use the strength of your full body to sing.

54

tuning dissonance

Slowly (♩ = 72)

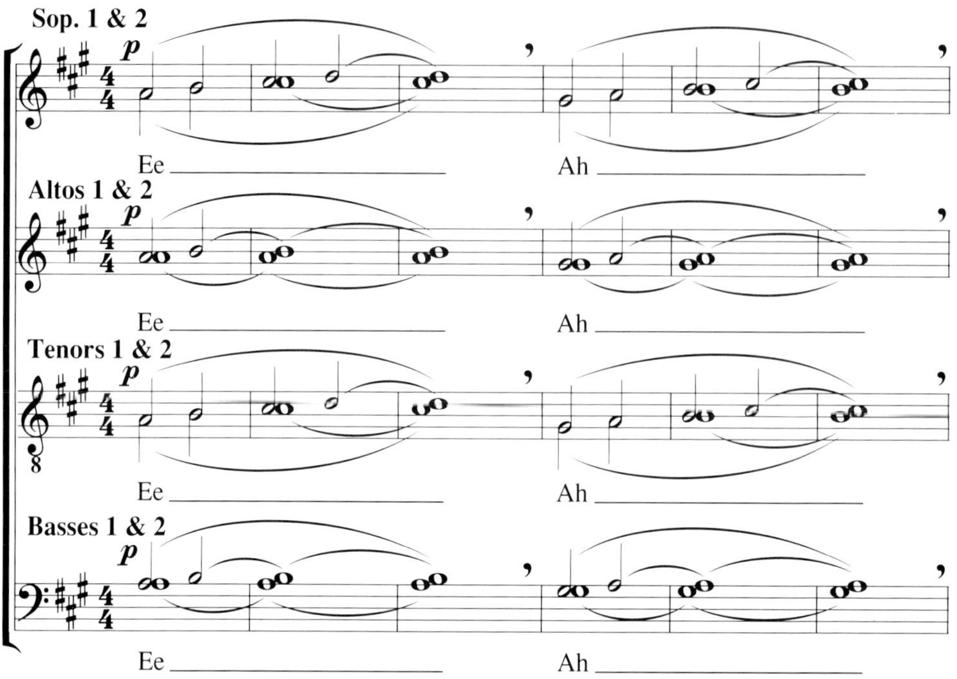

Sop. 1 & 2
p
Ee
Ah
Altos 1 & 2
p
Ee
Ah
Tenors 1 & 2
p
Ee
Ah
Basses 1 & 2
p
Ee
Ah

Oh
U
Oh
U
Oh
U
Oh
U

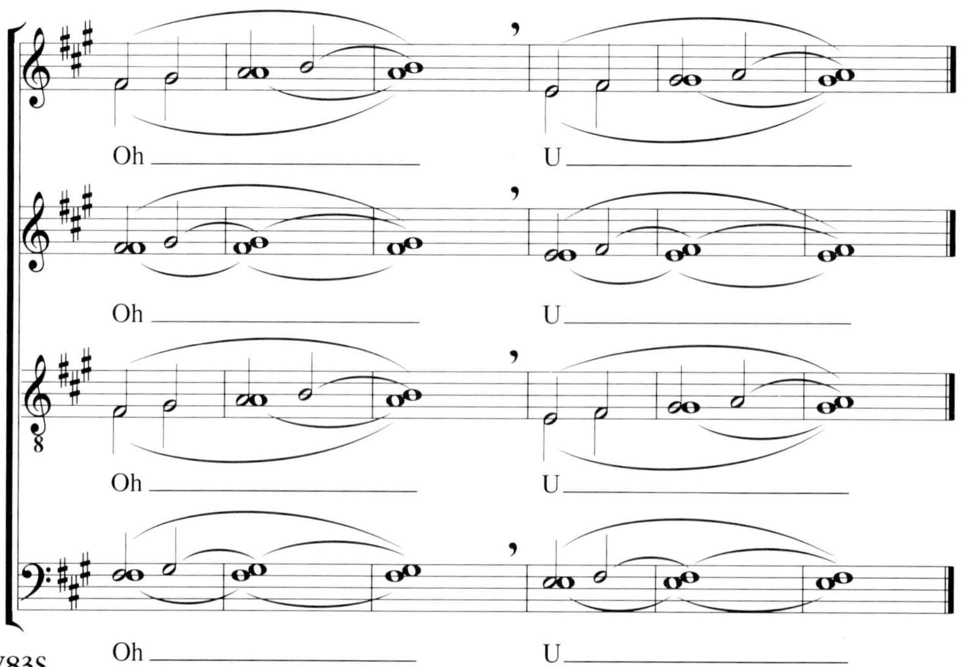

TIPS

A. Tune your long pitch carefully and then keep the pitch steady.

B. Tune with the accuracy of a laser.

C. Each singer's voice is a different size from their neighbor's. Each singer must be responsible for helping to maintain a balance within their own section and the choir as a whole.

Moderately (♩ = 88)

1. Ah dee, ah day, ah dō, ah du, ah dee, ah day, ah dō. Ah
2. Ah nee, ah nay, ah nō, ah nu, ah nee, ah nay, ah nō. Ah

TIPS

A. Sing the consonant at the beginning of a syllable at the same pitch as the vowel of that syllable:

B. Center the pitch of each note. The tuning of "mi" and "ti" should sound slightly sharp.

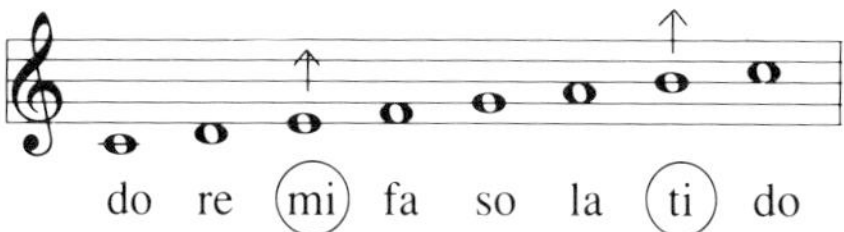

56

dim. = *diminuendo* = gradually softer = ⟩

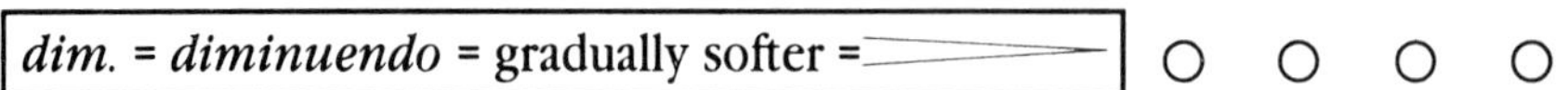

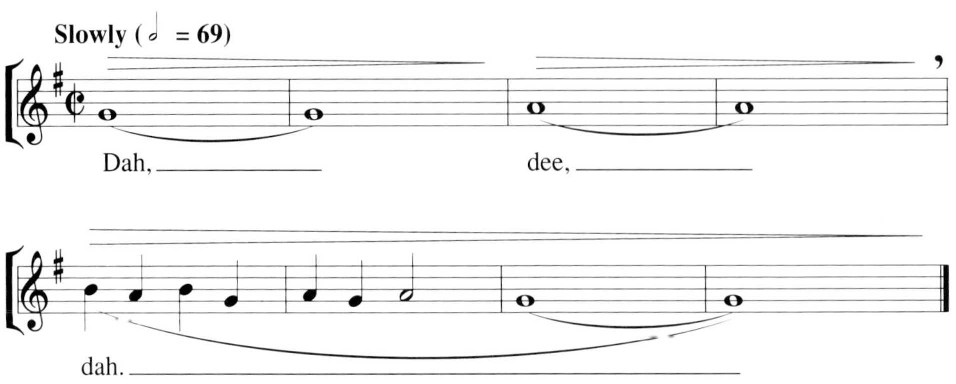

TIPS

A. ***Dim.*** **means a** **gradual** **change in dynamics. To even out the** ***dim.*****, imagine a large circle at the beginning of each** ***dim.*** **Imagine the circle gradually getting smaller and smaller during the** ***dim.*****:**

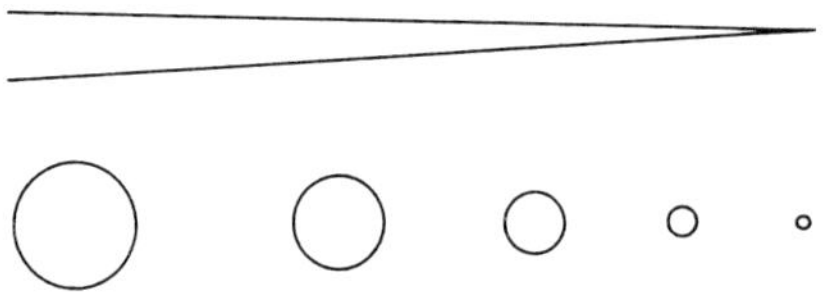

B. Start loud enough so that you have room to get softer.

C. Do not close your mouth to soften the sound; this would change the quality of sound and the tuning.

D. Keep the intensity to the end of the ***dim.*** **as you soften:**

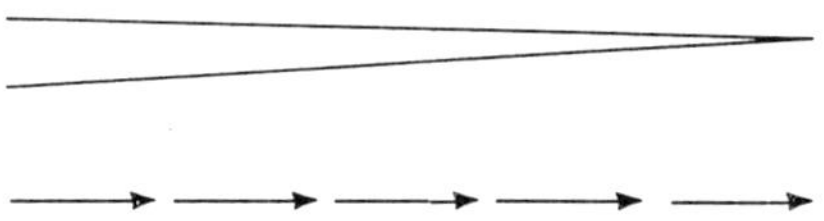

57

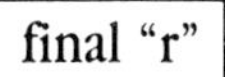
final "r"

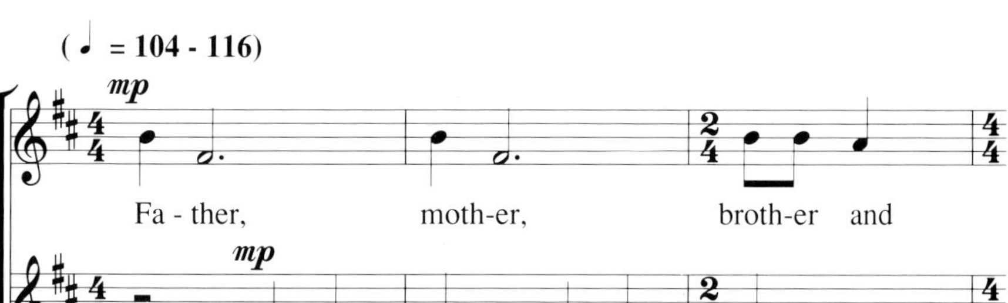
(♩ = 104 - 116)
mp
Part 1
Fa - ther, moth-er, broth-er and
mp
Part 2
Fa - ther, moth-er,

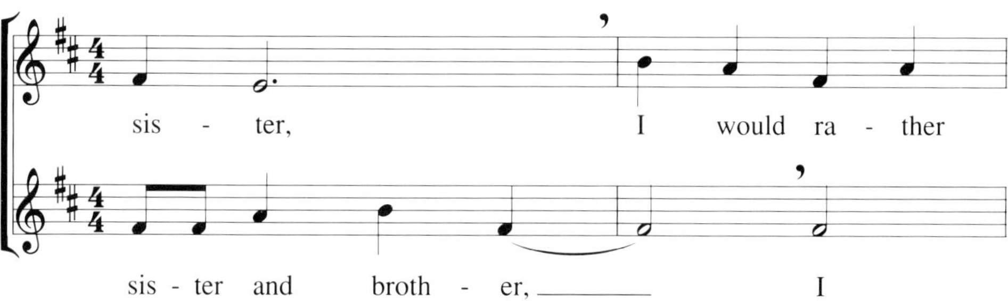
sis - ter, I would ra - ther
sis - ter and broth - er, I

leave this place and nev-er, nev-er re - turn.
would nev - er re - turn.

TIPS

A. "R" is not a pleasant sound. Omit "r" at the end of a word. Sing a neutral "uh" instead of "er":

fa-thuh mo-thuh bro-thuh sis-tuh

B. Keep your jaw down for "r"; it is very difficult to produce the nasty "rrr" sound when the jaw is down.

C. When we speak, we emphasize certain syllables to give more importance to those syllables:

I would ra - ther leave this place.	*I would ra - ther leave this place*
(boring, wooden difficult to understand)	(interesting, easier to understand)

In music, the strong syllable usually falls on a strong beat. Emphasize the strong syllables; lighten the weak syllables:

fa-ther moth-er broth-er sis-ter

D. During rehearsals, cross out the final "r" on your music as a reminder.

Fa - ther

REMINDER **Breathe in to the lower part of the back.**

58

warming up the upper part of the range

○ ○ ○ ○ ○

u = sounds like the "oo" in moon

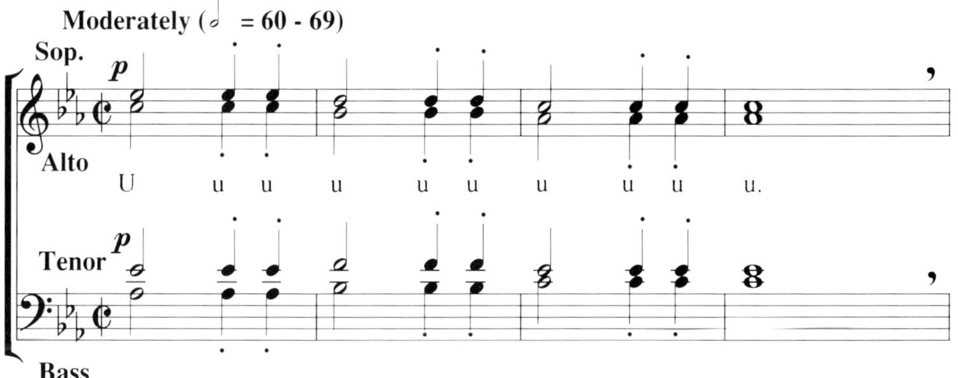

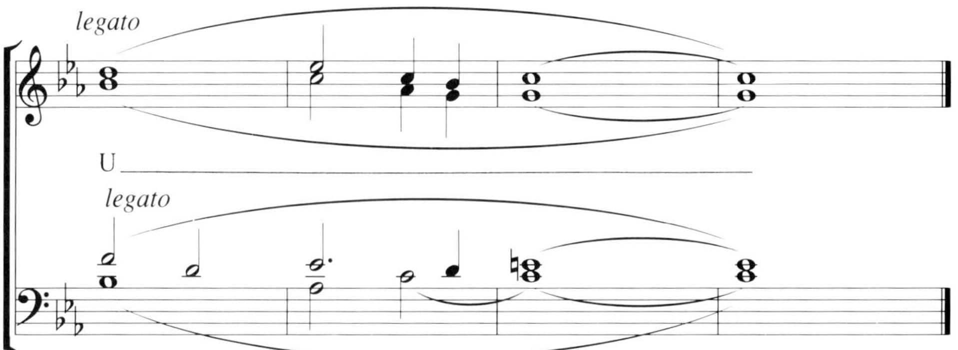

TIPS

A. Increase the intensity of the air slightly for higher pitches. Keep your throat relaxed.

B. Sing softly to gradually warm up the higher pitches.

C. Keep the tone light. Focus the sound in the center of the forehead.

D. Warm up the tone on the longer notes. Focus the tone for staccato.

59

precision in diction

○ ○ ○ ○ ○

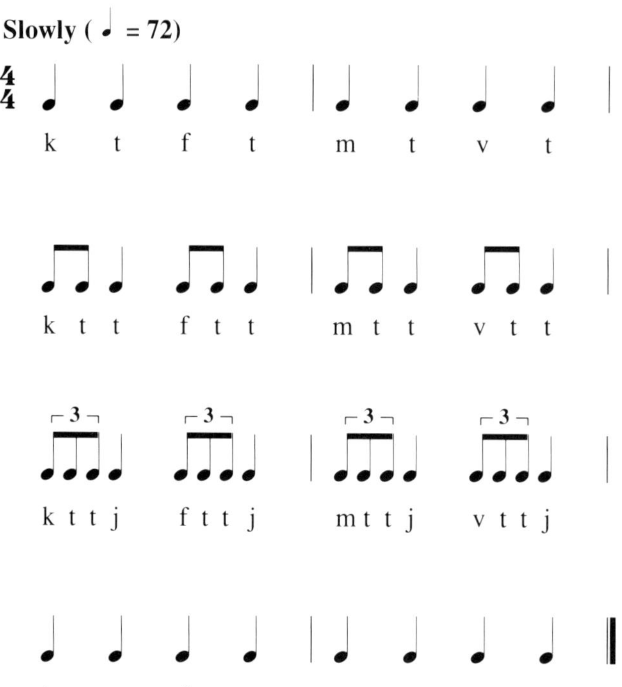

TIPS

A. Keep the beat precise.

B. Relax the throat. Let the tummy muscles do the work.

C. Do not use excess head movement. Some singers may make a slight natural movement as they sing without hurting the precision but the movement should not be obvious.

D. Say the consonants as if you were communicating a very important message in an alien language.

60 extending the range down

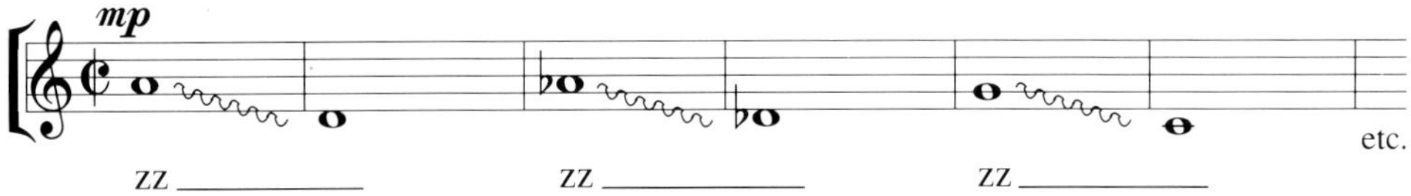

TIPS

A. Keep your teeth slightly apart and your jaw relaxed. Do not point your head down as the pitch descends.

B. Let the sound buzz; it will not be a pleasant, high-quality sound but it will get everything vibrating.

C. Keep the buzz uniform during the *glissando*. Even out the tone throughout this part of your range.

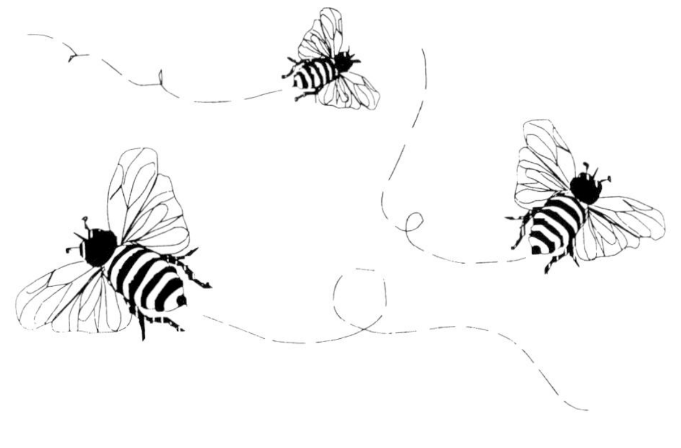

REMINDER **For a healthy voice, drink plenty of water each day.**

61

cresc., dim.

Moderately (♩ = 108)
Part 1
Part 2
mp
f
Glo - ri - a, glo-ri-a, glo-ri-a,
Glo - ri-a, glo-ri-a, glo -
glo - ri - a. Glo - ri - a, glo - ri - a.
- ri - a, glo-ri-a. Glo - ri - a, glo - ri - a.

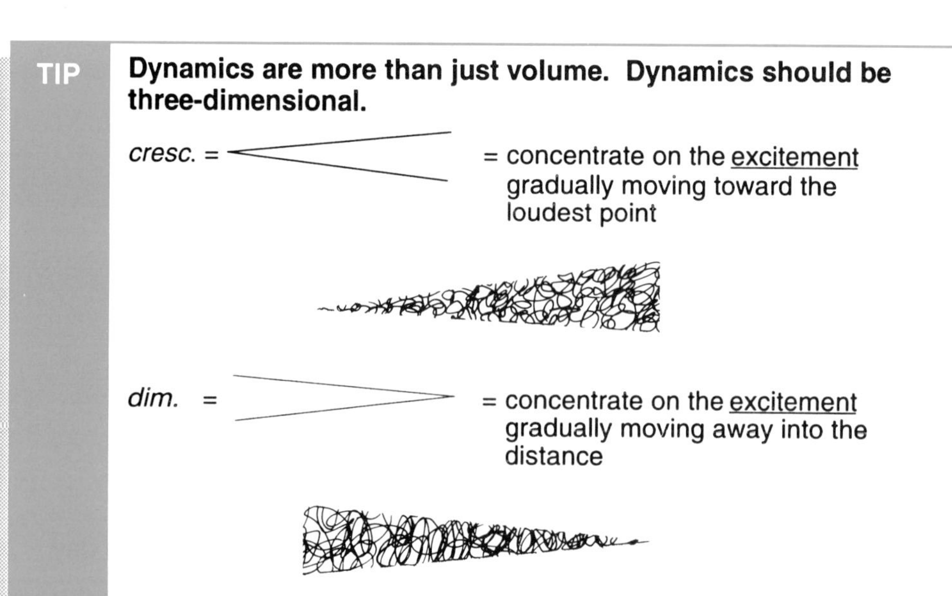
TIP
Dynamics are more than just volume. Dynamics should be three-dimensional.
cresc. =
= concentrate on the excitement gradually moving toward the loudest point
dim. =
= concentrate on the excitement gradually moving away into the distance

62

accel., rit

○ ○ ○ ○ ○

rit. = *ritardando* = gradually slower
accel. = *accelerando* = gradually faster

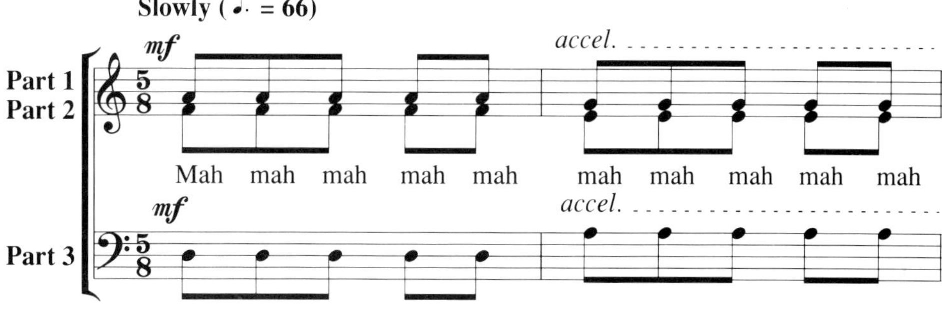

TIPS

A. **Pace the change of speed. The tempo should not <u>suddenly</u> slow down or speed up.**

B. **Watch the conductor carefully for each *rit.* and *accel.* Memorize that part of the music.**

63

short "o"

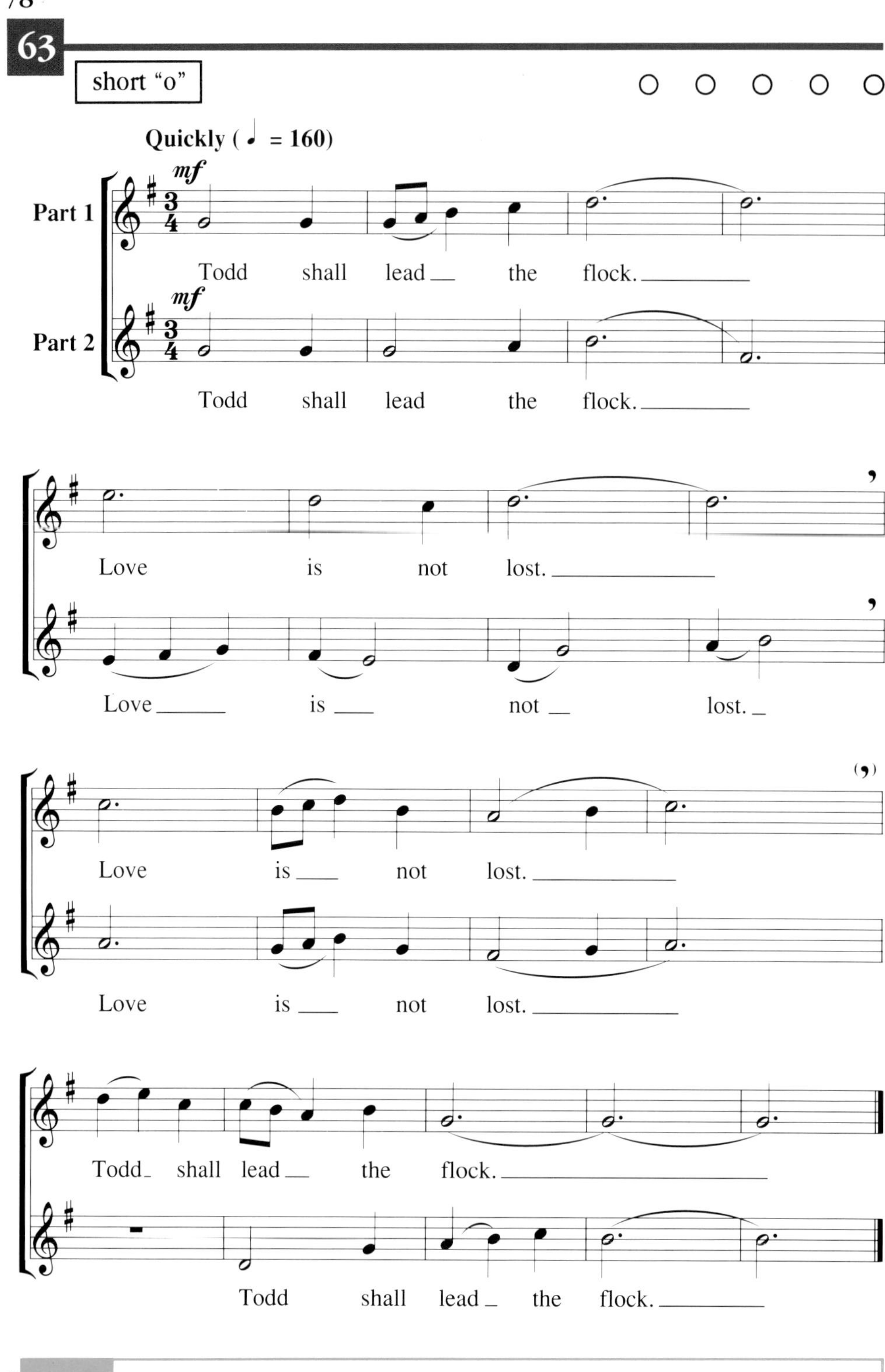

TIP For short "o," sing "ah."

64

feel the strength of the diaphragm

1) Face a chairback or wall;
2) Place your hands at a comfortable position on the chairback or wall (about waist height);
3) Move your feet back from the chair or wall;
4) Lean toward the chair until you can feel the weight of your body pressing against your tummy.

TIPS

A. Sing this warmup in the position shown above so that you can feel the muscles in your tummy. Repeat in a standing position. Alternate between the two positions.

B. Do not continue for too long; build up the stamina gradually.

C. Keep the low pitches light; let the resonance of the lower pitches gently glide up into the higher pitches. Do not try to push any resonance from the chest upward into higher pitches.

65

y

Moderately (♩ = 66 - 80)

TIPS

A. Form the "y" as a quick glide at the front of your mouth.

B. Let your tummy bounce you up to the higher note.

C. Think of the sound as a spinning baseball:

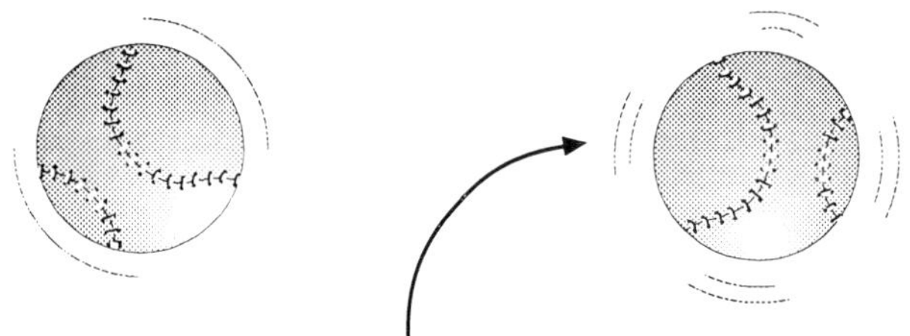

The ball is slowly spinning, suspended in the air.

Suddenly add some speed to the spin for the higher pitch

Try not to anticipate the sudden leap early. Imagine you are the pitcher trying to "fake out" the batter by releasing the ball unexpectedly.

REMINDER

Think of your body as a tree. Use the strength of your full body to sing.

66

sustained note at end of a phrase

○ ○ ○ ○ ○

TIPS

A. **Sustained notes provide an opportunity to make the vowel sound as beautiful as possible.**

B. **Pace your air carefully. When you reach the final note of the phrase, spin the sound forward.**

C. **The second phrase will need more control because:**

- **You are fresher for the first phrase;**
- **There are more consonants in the second phrase and consonants need more air.**

D. **If you start to run out of air:**

- **Put more energy into your singing;**
- **Let the momentum carry you to the end of the phrase.**

67

high glides

Very slowly (♩ = 52)

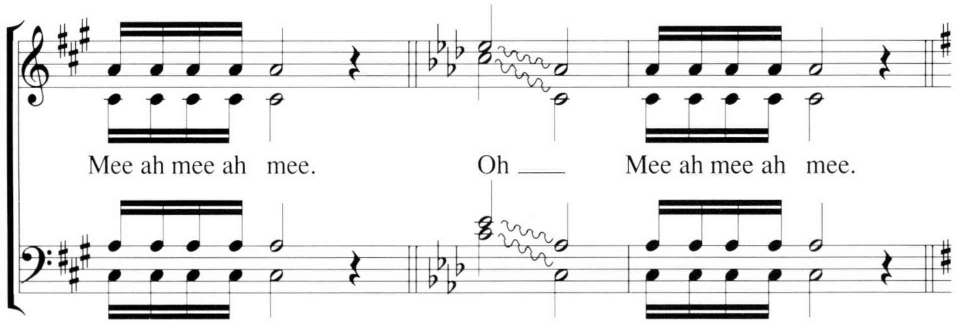

TIPS

A. Let your voice slide slowly through all the pitches "between the cracks."

B. Even out the sound in the areas where your voice tends to"skip" rather than moving in a continuous glide.

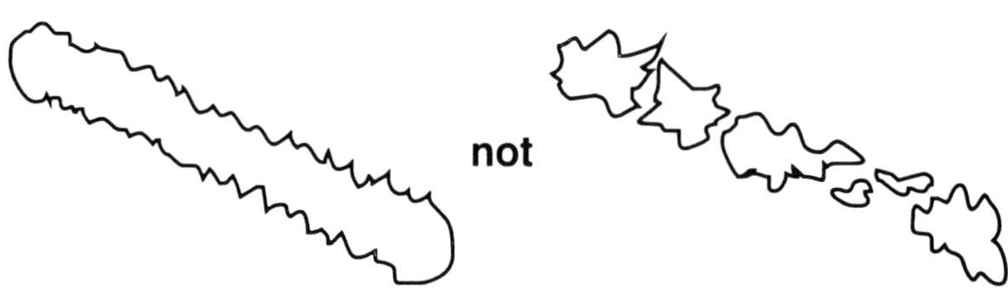

C. Each vowel needs to be warmed up separately. When the "ah" is working well, try "oh," "eh," "ee" or "u."

REMINDER

For high pitches, drop the jaw and expand the throat.

68

emphasizing the right syllable

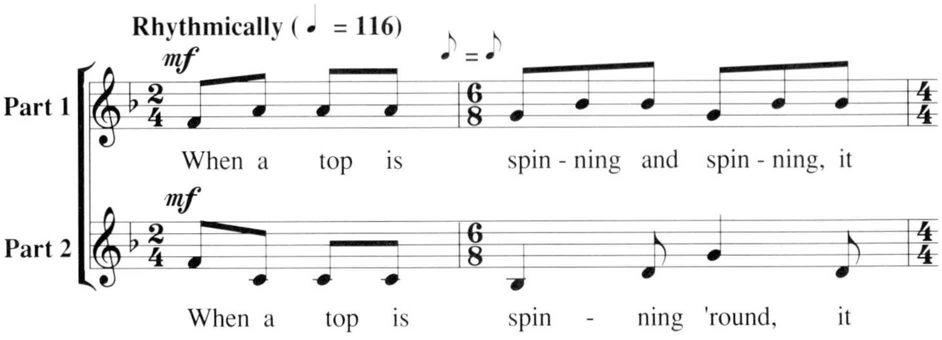

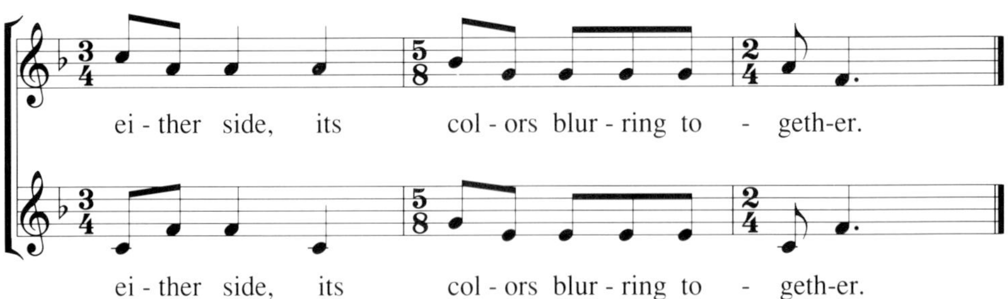

TIPS

A. For rhythmic music, emphasize the first note in every grouping:

B. When we speak, the pitch of our voices moves up and down slightly. Sometimes the pitch of the music will go against the direction of the natural speaking inflection:

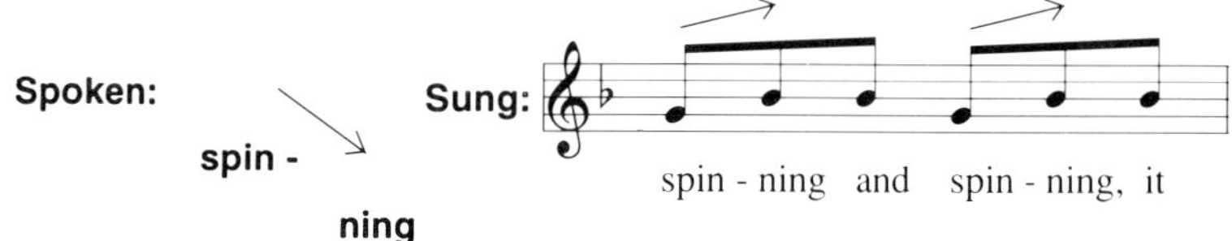

The important syllable will need a bit more emphasis.

C. Sometimes a composer like Stravinsky will "play" with the words and put the weak syllables on the strong beats to add rhythmic interest to the music. In a case like this, emphasize the important beats of the music, not the important syllables of the words.

69

tuning thirds and leading tones in chords

○ ○ ○ ○ ○

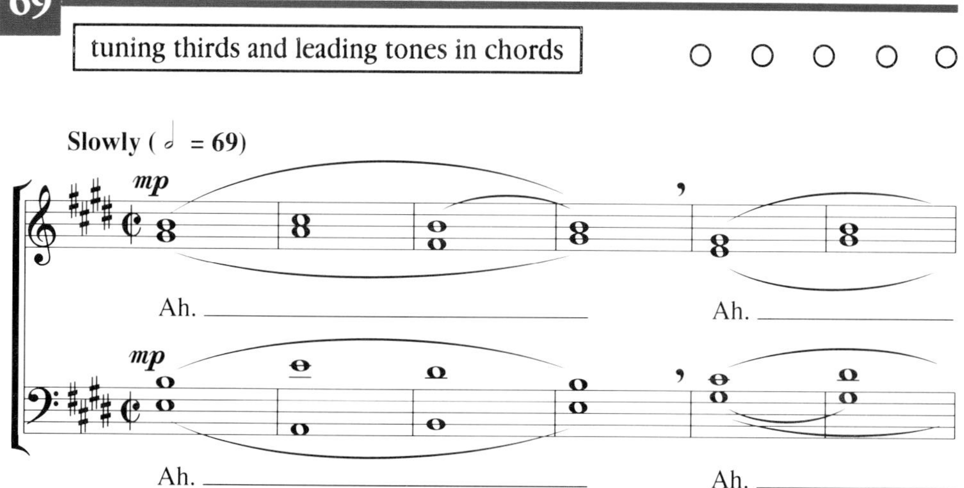

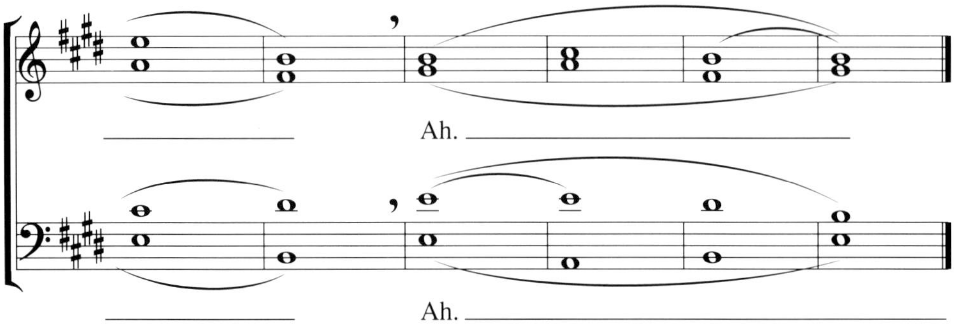

TIPS

A. Identify which chords do not sound in tune.

B. Who is singing the third of each chord?

The third of a minor chord is lower than the third of a major chord:

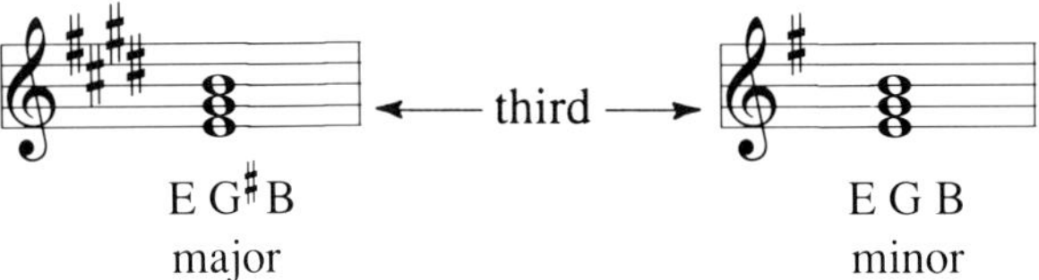

In a major chord, is the third tuned high enough?

In a minor chord, is the third tuned low enough?

C. Is the leading tone sharp enough? It should sound as if it is leading toward the tonic even when it does not move to the tonic right away.

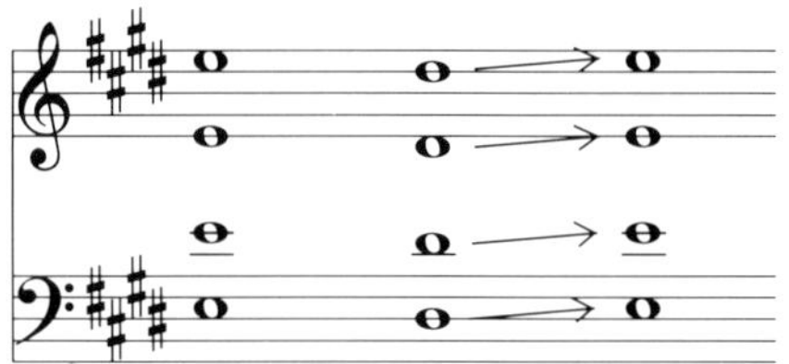

D. Circle out-of-tune pitches in your concert repertoire as a reminder to listen carefully.

70

shaping the phrase

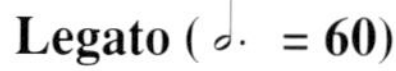

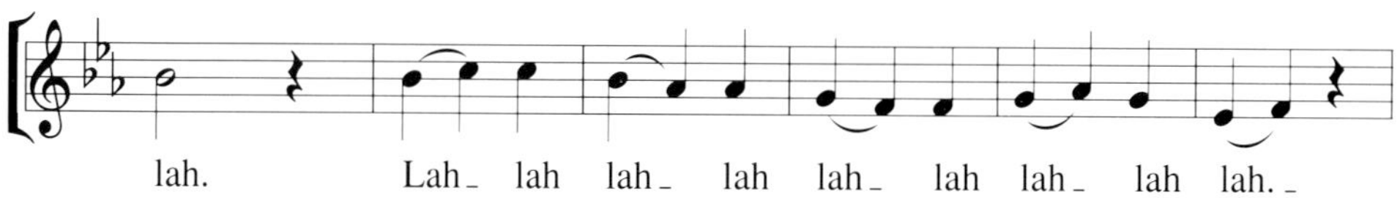

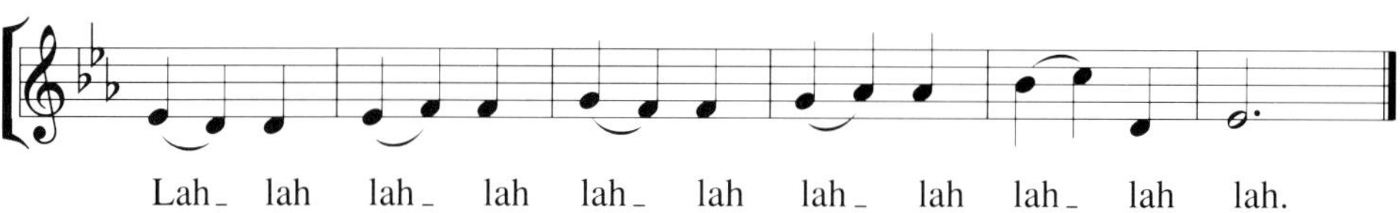

TIPS

A. Every piece of music has a climax; every section of that piece has a climax; every phrase has a climax:

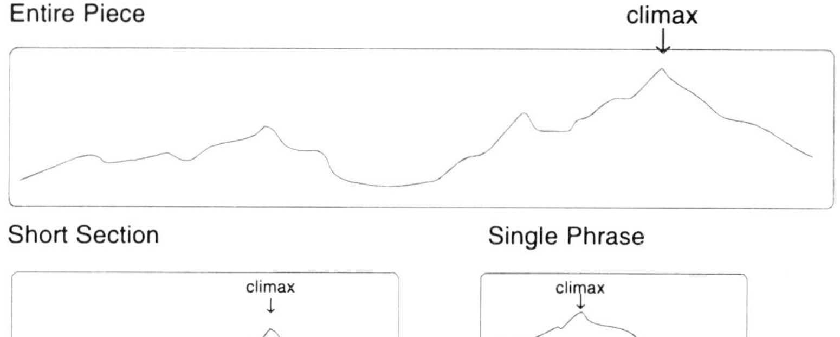

Climaxes come in all shapes and sizes.

B. A climax can be anywhere in a phrase. In this warmup, the highest pitches are at the climaxes.

C. Feel how the energy moves toward the climax and then slowly relaxes.

71

no excess sound in final consonants

At a steady tempo (♩ = 92)

Sop. div.
mf
Stop moan-ing. Keep
Alto
mf
Stop moan-ing. Keep
Tenor
mf
Stop moan-ing. Keep
Bass div.
mf
Stop moan-ing. Keep
mov-ing. Troub-le through-out the land.
mov-ing. Troub-le through-out the land.
mov-ing. Troub-le through-out the land.
mov-ing. Troub-le through-out the land.

TIPS

A. Do not add an extra vocal syllable after the consonant:

Sto___p **not** *Sto___puh*

B. Do not breathe during <u>every</u> rest.

C. Sometimes the publisher may place a consonant with the preceding syllable for correct hyphenation, but you should always sing the consonant at the same pitch as the vowel that follows:

moan - ing = moa - ning

mov - ing = mo - ving

72

vowels modified by a final "n"

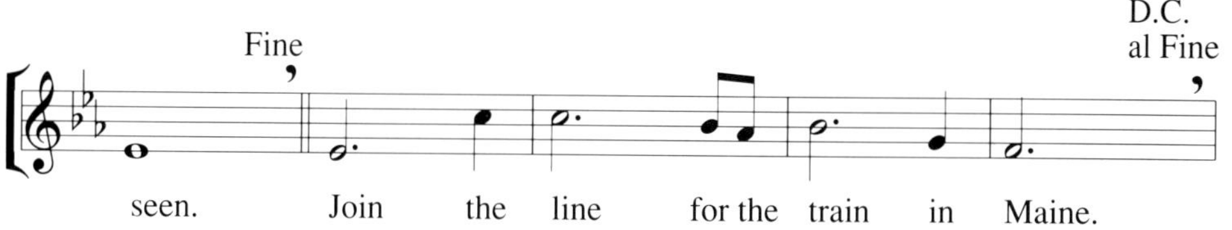

TIPS

A. Stretch out the pure vowel until the last possible moment.

B. Do not start closing your mouth early to anticipate the "n."

C. Practice "n" words without the "n" first. Then repeat with the "n" added as late as possible.

73

pr tr fr

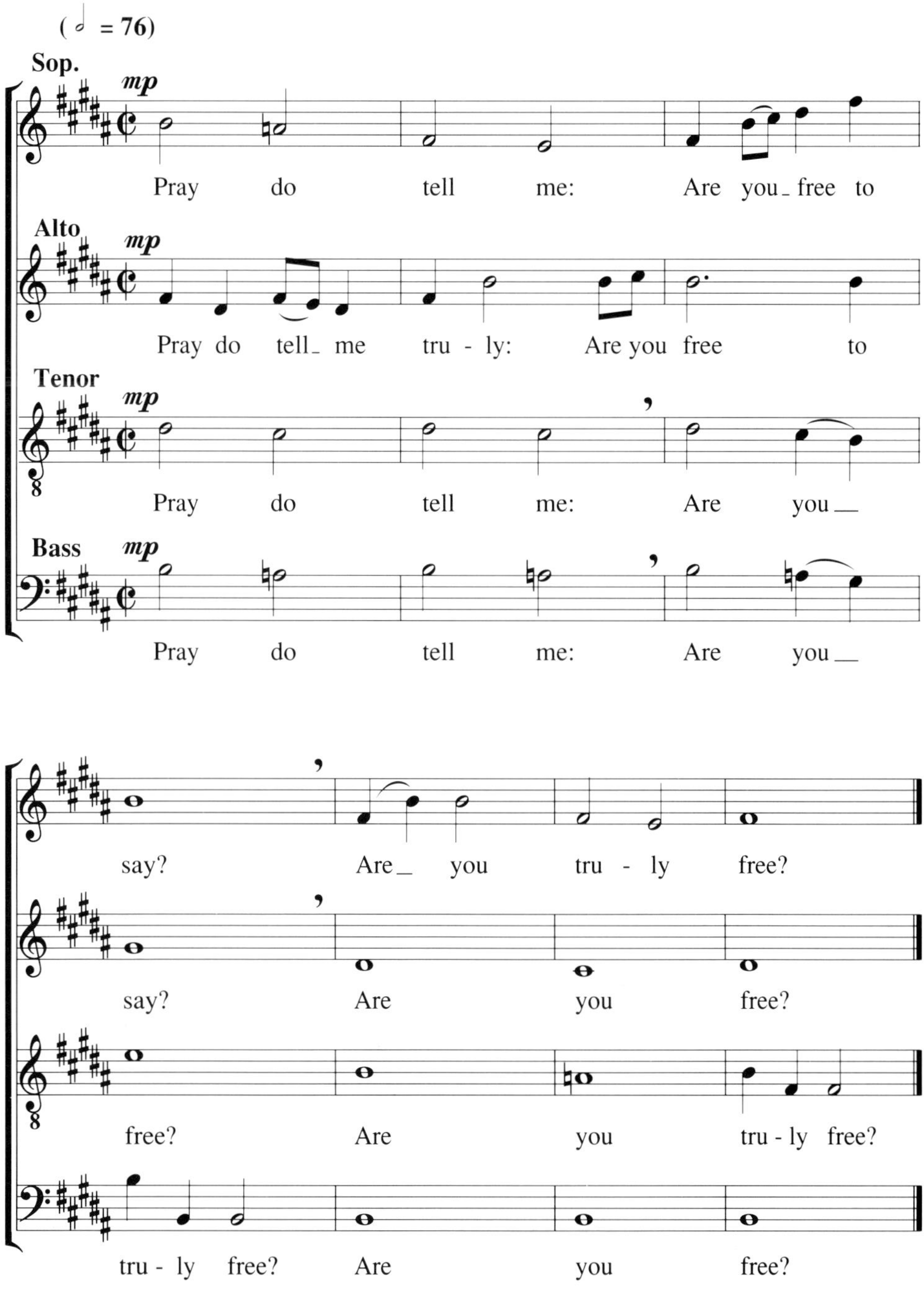

(𝅗𝅥 = 76)

Sop. *mp*

Pray do tell me: Are you free to

Alto *mp*

Pray do tell_ me tru - ly: Are you free to

Tenor *mp*

Pray do tell me: Are you_

Bass *mp*

Pray do tell me: Are you_

TIPS

A. Flip the "r" very lightly with your tongue like the beginning of a soft purr.

B. The flipped "r" is easier if you make the preceding consonant very short and light.

REMINDER

Think of your body as a tree. Use the strength of your full body to sing.

74

final consonant/initial vowel

○ ○ ○ ○ ○

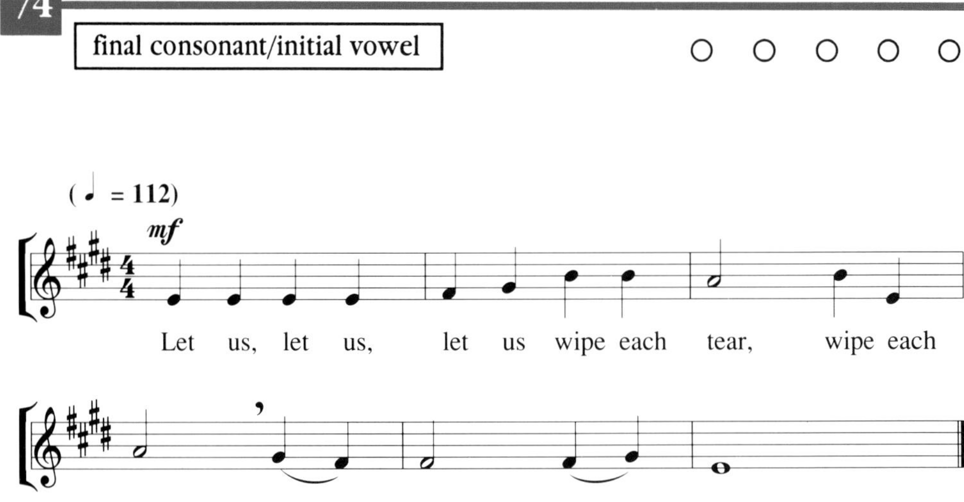

TIPS

A. When one word ends with a consonant and the next word begins with a vowel, leave a very small space after the final consonant of the first word.

let us ≠ lettuce

wipe each ≠ why peach?

at once ≠ a twonce *(What is a "twonce," anyway?)*

B. Place the consonant at the same pitch as the vowel of that same syllable.

SECOND YEAR PROGRESS CHART

Circle the appropriate number:

1 - understands the skill
2 - can do the skill
3 - some improvement shown
4 - good progress
5 - excellent progress
6 - remembers consistently

Singers in Position - use full body (like a tree)	1 2 3 4 5 6
38. drop the jaw	1 2 3 4 5 6
39. rhythmic diction - consonants at front of mouth	1 2 3 4 5 6
- emphasis on first eighth of each grouping	1 2 3 4 5 6
40. bl cl gl fl pl sl	1 2 3 4 5 6
41. five vowel workout	1 2 3 4 5 6
42. gliding in mid-range	1 2 3 4 5 6
Quick check: Early morning hum	1 2 3 4 5 6
43. slurs	1 2 3 4 5 6
- ribcage up for singing	1 2 3 4 5 6
44. changing tempo suddenly	1 2 3 4 5 6
45. sk sp squ st	1 2 3 4 5 6
- think of music as communication	1 2 3 4 5 6
46. tuning a melody with framework pitches	1 2 3 4 5 6
47. short "a"	1 2 3 4 5 6
48. extending your range up	
- drop jaw; open throat	1 2 3 4 5 6
- sing lightly; use momentum of phrase	1 2 3 4 5 6
49. syncopation	1 2 3 4 5 6
50. w wh	1 2 3 4 5 6
Quick check: Drinking water?	1 2 3 4 5 6
51. alternating long and short breaks for breaths	1 2 3 4 5 6
- long breaths: breathe in through soles of feet	1 2 3 4 5 6
- short breaths: breathe in from tummy	1 2 3 4 5 6
52. oy	1 2 3 4 5 6
53. terraced dynamics	1 2 3 4 5 6
54. tuning dissonance	1 2 3 4 5 6
55. final vowel/initial consonant	1 2 3 4 5 6
56. *dim.*	1 2 3 4 5 6
57. final "r"	1 2 3 4 5 6

58. warming up the upper part of the range	
- increase the intensity of the air	1 2 3 4 5 6
- sing softly	1 2 3 4 5 6
- keep the tone light	1 2 3 4 5 6
- focus the sound in the center of the forehead	1 2 3 4 5 6
Quick check: Posture?	1 2 3 4 5 6
59. precision in diction - no excess head movement	1 2 3 4 5 6
60. extending the range down - even out the sound	1 2 3 4 5 6
61. *cresc., dim.*	1 2 3 4 5 6
62. *accel., rit.*	1 2 3 4 5 6
63. short "o"	1 2 3 4 5 6
64. feel the strength of the diaphragm	1 2 3 4 5 6
65. y	1 2 3 4 5 6
- bounce up for leaps	1 2 3 4 5 6
66. sustained note at end of phrase	1 2 3 4 5 6
67. high glides - even out the sound	1 2 3 4 5 6
68. emphasizing the right syllable	1 2 3 4 5 6
Quick check: Breathing?	1 2 3 4 5 6
69. tuning thirds and leading tones in chords	1 2 3 4 5 6
70. shaping the phrase (climaxes)	1 2 3 4 5 6
71. no excess sound in final consonants	1 2 3 4 5 6
72. vowels modified by a final "n"	1 2 3 4 5 6
73. pr tr fr	1 2 3 4 5 6
74. final consonant/initial vowel	1 2 3 4 5 6
◆ ◆ **CONGRATULATIONS!** ◆ ◆	

Index

accel. - 77
accent - 5
balancing voices - 33, 69
breathing - 5, 8, 10-14, 28-30, 38, 50, 56, 64, 73, 79, 81, 90
- practice - 5, 8, 10, 27-28, 30, 64, 81, 88
- strengthen tummy muscles - 5, 8, 79
- practice different phrase lengths - 10, 30, 33
breathiness - 34, *see* resonance, forward placement
chin - 23
circle of sound - 7, 23, 56
consonants - 6, 51-52, 69, 88-90, 92
- b - 5; practice - 5-6, 51, 66
- bl - 52-53
- c - *see* k
- ch - 43; practice - 43, 69
- cl - 52-53
- d - 9; practice - 9-10, 19, 39, 45, 51, 62, 66, 69
- f - 26; practice - 26, 55, 64, 74
- fl - 52-53
- fr - 91-92
- g - 32; practice - 32, 51
- gl - 52-53, 76
- h - 43
- j - 9; practice - 9, 69, 74
- k - 32; practice - 32, 51, 74
- l - 17; practice - 17, 55, 78
- m - 7, 16, 21, 26-27, 46, 50-51, 54, 74
- additional practice - 79, 82
- n - 17, 90; practice - 17, 69, 90
- p - 5; practice - 5-6, 19, 30, 51, 88
- pl - 52-53
- pr - 91-92
- r - 71-72, 91-92
- s - 26, 58; practice - 26, 55
- sh - 26
- sl - 52-53
- sp sk st squ - 58
- t - 9; practice - 9, 15, 19, 51, 74, 78
- th - 37, 43; practice - 37, 43, 66
- tr - 91-92
- v - 37; practice - 37, 66, 74
- w wh - 63
- y - 80; practice - 7, 80
- z - 45
cut-off - 19-20, 27-28, 39, 42, 88-90
- practice 10, 19, 27, 30, 39, 42, 44, 54, 58, 64, 87-88
diction - 6, 52, 58, 69, 74, 92, *see* vowels, consonants
diphthong - 42-43
- ō - 20-21, 24; practice - 20, 24, 38, 64, 66, 69
- ā - 36, 55; practice - 36, 38, 42, 44-45, 55, 69
- oy - 65
dissonance - 68
dynamics - *forte* - 7, 28-29, 33
- *piano* - 7, 38, *see* breathing, posture, forward placement, resonance
- *cresc.* - 27, 40-41, 76
- terraced - 66-67; practice 18, 25, 66, 88
- *dim.* - 70, 76
energy - drink water - 9
- balanced body - 4, 13
- head in position - 8
flat - *see* tuning
flexibility - *see* leaps
- practice runs - 24-25, 39, 61
- practice unusual or changing time signatures - 18, 51, 77, 84
forward placement - 16, 29, 31, 34, 38, 45, 52

glides - 50, 55, 75, 82-83
hear own voice - 32, 41, 54
high pitches - 61, 73, 82-83, *see* posture
humming - *see* consonants: m
jaw - *see* mouth open
leaps - 80; practice - 27, 31, 38, 69, 80
legato - 6, 15, 25; practice - 6, 15, 20, 25
lips - position - 5, 21, 31-32, 63
- practice - 5, 20, 30-31, 63, 77, 79
low pitches - 55-56, 75, 79, *see* posture
- practice - 7, 36, 42, 55, 60, 62, 71, 75, 79
mouth open - 7, 8, 15, 23, 29, 36, 39, 50-51, 61, 70, 72, 75
phrasing - 10-13, 27-28, 30, 39, 40-41, 52-53, 61, 81, 87, *see legato*
- additional practice - 25, 66, 78, 88
- practice different phrase lengths - 10, 30, 33
posture - 4, 8, 13-14, 50
precision - 6, 74, *see* posture, tongue, lips
projection - 46, *see* forward placement, resonance
relaxation - 4-5, 8, 14, 18, 50
resonance - 16-17, 21, 27, 29, 34, 37, 41, 45, 79
- glides - 55, 75, 82-83
- additional practice - *see* consonant m
rhythmic singing - 18-19, 51-52, 62, 72, 84-85
- practice - 9-10, 14, 18, 30, 43, 51, 57, 62, 71, 77, 84
rit. - 77
sharp - *see* tuning
slurs - 55-56
stamina - 58, 79, *see* posture, vocal health, breathing, phrasing
sustained notes - 20, 22-23, 35, 39, 44, 81
- additional practice - 66, 70, 85
tempo - 57, 77
throat - 8, 18, 61, 73-74
tone quality - *see* vowels, forward placement, sustained notes
- practice glides - 55, 75, 82-83
tongue - 9, 15, 17, 32, 37, 43, 62
- practice - 9-10, 14, 17, 19, 32, 39, 55, 60, 62, 65, 74, 81
tuning - 15, 17, 23, 26, 46, 56, 69, 70, 85-86, 90, 92, *see* vowels, breathing
- flat - 23, 38, 56
- sharp - 23, *see* relaxation
- melodic - 17, 59, 69, 86
- harmonic - 22-23, 35, 44, 85-86
- dissonance - 68-69
- *piano* - 38, 70
vocal health - 9, 43
vowels - 6-7, 41, 54, 63, 69, 81, 83, 90, 92
- practice - 54, 63, 90, *see* sustained notes
- ah - 6-7; practice - 6-7, 9-10, 15-17, 22, 25, 27, 35, 38 -39, 44, 46, 50, 55, 68, 70, 85, 87
- ee - 15, 24; practice - 15-16, 19, 22, 24, 35, 46, 58-59, 64, 68-70, 82
- eh - 36
- long "a" - 36; practice - 36, 38, 42, 44-45, 69
- long "o" - 20-21, 24; practice - 20, 24, 38, 64, 66, 69
- oh - 20, 24, 65; practice -22, 24, 35, 44, 46, 68, 76, 80
- short "a" - 60
- short "o" - 78; practice - 19, 78
- u - 31; practice - 31, 35, 38, 44, 52, 68-69, 73, 81